When Spirit Speaks

Denise Burroughs

1nkd
Publishing

When Spirit Speaks

Denise Burroughs

InkEd
Publisher

Published by Inkd Publishing LLC 2024

254 SW Range Ave., Madison FL 32340

Library of Congress Control Number: 2024945707

ISBN: 979-8-9907868-9-9(hc)

ISBN: 979-8-9913917-0-2(e)

ISBN: 979-8-9913917-1-9(p)

To the Spirits
Who inspired me to write this book.
Without your presence in this world
This book would never have come to pass

In Loving Memory of
Mitchell Kingston
My friend and Team member, Always

*IN A WORLD FULL OF DARKNESS THERE IS EVIL,
AND WHEN THE DOORS ARE OPENED
THE NIGHTMARES BEGIN*

When Spirit Speaks

Contents

Foreword

April Balsamo Davis

Little did I know that my chance meeting with Denise Burroughs would turn into a friendship, and later a professional relationship. I always believed in the existence of the spirit world to some extent, but I knew little about the paranormal and had never given any thought to what a medium could do. I had the opportunity to accompany Denise and her team on several paranormal investigations and witnessed her gifts firsthand. She was able to sense and describe details of the spirits in a location before the equipment was set up to record data. It was nothing short of incredible. I believe that the compassion that she has for both the people experiencing paranormal activity and the spirits that she encounters is one of her greatest strengths.

When Denise first approached me about editing this book, I was excited about the prospect. In my work as a freelance editor, it is rare that I get to work on a project as unique as this one. The stories contained in the pages of *When Spirit Speaks* are the real-life stories of the paranormal encounters that Denise Burroughs has experienced or investigated over the years. She is a great storyteller, and the book might just change your perspective on what you thought you knew about spirits. I'm sure you will enjoy reading it.

April Balsamo Davis

Introduction

What was once thought to be my imaginary playmate ended up changing my life. I had a gift to communicate with spirits. I was fascinated by this ability to see, hear, and feel the energy from those that have passed on. I kept pushing myself to get a deeper understanding of my abilities. It is what goes bump in the night that caught my attention, and from that moment on I never looked back.

Spirit and the paranormal always seemed natural to me. I do not walk alone in this world. I am guided by my spirit guide who made itself known to me at a young age. Years later I realized the importance of this spirit guide in my life and in my future calling. My spirit guide is a huge part of this journey. My heart, my soul, and my feelings are guided gently by a sense. I am drawn to people that are in need. I've always been able to pick up on things but haven't necessarily listened to that inner self.

I had to adjust my life, my mind, and my thoughts to

accommodate my new friends from the afterlife. Challenging at times, yes, but also gratifying. I learned to use my ability to communicate with spirits not only to help the living, but to help those who were no longer here; to either help them move on, or to understand the attachments they still have in the physical world. My conversations with spirits are no different than when I speak to a living person. The only difference is that they don't respond in the same way, making the conversation more one-sided.

In my travels I've had a chance to meet people from all walks of life, many who have shared the same kind of experiences that I have. Let's face it, we all have that natural built-in ability to protect ourselves. Some need more time to learn how to use it.

I have made many places my home. As I moved around the country I did a lot of soul searching; I needed to understand. I wanted more. The paranormal was everywhere, but not talked about much. I grew up in the '70s and '80s. The topic was still on the hush, but it was out there hidden. Yes, we did have 800 hotlines for psychic advice, private readings, and tea leaves.

I had my tea leaves read by an English woman named Laura. It's crazy looking back on it now. She told me so much about myself and my potential. She seemed to look right into me. After every reading she would tell me "You're going to go far. You will help many along the way. You're special." I thought to myself, *she got all that from tea?*

Laura was talented and truly amazing. She helped me to understand life and to accept my own gifts at a young age. She knew that, although I went to her for guidance, I just needed to trust and accept. I had to get focused. Looking back, I remember so much, all the visitations, dreams, and more. It was my world beginning to unfold.

I finally settled back to my roots and the state I call home and accepted all of this in my life. I use my gift to help people, like I was guided to all those years past. It felt natural once I accepted myself and stopped worrying about what anyone thought. Once that door opened, it never closed. My light was on and it was staying on.

Chapter 1

Hollywood, Florida

I was working the night shift at a local hospital in South Florida. I will not divulge the name for privacy reasons. The morgue was where I always ended up going because no one else wanted to do it. It was here that I saw my first apparition. *Wow!* was all I could say. It energized my light

One night I was called to the floor to get a patient who had passed away. It was a Saturday night. A lot of people had called out and there just wasn't enough staff. I really had no choice, so I headed to the morgue with the deceased. I had to take the elevator. It was weird because the elevator stopped not once, but twice between floors. I was a wreck. I just wanted off and out of that elevator. The glitches were short-lived, and I made it to the ground floor. I walked down a long hallway and finally to the exit to where the morgue was located. At the time the morgue was detached from the main hospital. I was praying that the door was unlocked, or I would need to call and wait for security to come and open the door.

As I entered the room it was cold and dark, only small lights on. I did what I went there to do and, as I was leaving, I spotted a small crib-like bed. I felt deep sadness. I just knew it was a small child. I turned around and as I was walking out, I got so cold I froze in the spot I was standing in. I couldn't move. My hair was standing up on my body. I just stood there. I finally turned and there was a child with red hair wrapped in a beautiful green blanket gazing at me. I was frozen in place. We had no cell phones back then and there was no way to take a picture of what I saw. I just stared at her and then I finally ran out. I just needed to catch my breath. I was trying to think of how to explain this. My shift was over, and I went home.

I was supposed to be off the next day, but I was asked to work a four-hour shift. I wasn't busy, so I decided to head to the morgue. I was curious about the encounter from the day before, not only about what I saw and felt, but about that small crib. I went in like I normally do. The gurneys were all moved around. This room also had an autopsy room, which is always off limits. I walked toward the small bed; a sheet was over it. I just had to sneak a peek and look. I was shocked! It was the child I saw the day before, red hair and green blanket.

I felt so much sadness and so much pain. Then it hit me, the green blanket was not covering her. So, I covered her. As I covered her, it was a sign. Not sure why or how, but I felt at ease once I fixed her blanket.

I remember walking out and heading to the chapel, which is a place I often went to in the hospital. It was peaceful there.

I prayed for the child's family and asked God to give them peace. That first apparition was one of many in years to come.

Hollywood, Florida was the site of my first investigation. It started out as a crazy paranormal 101. I was about to begin and all I had was a flashlight and a cassette recorder. I felt ready to do this. It was my first home investigation, and I was quite nervous.

The woman that owned the home moved in after the previous owner passed away. She said everything was fine for about a month, then keys went missing and lights started flickering. The keys upset her because she missed a day of work, ripped the place apart, and didn't find her keys. She proceeded to tell me that later she went to the kitchen for a glass of water and the keys were on the floor in plain sight. She was horrified by that.

My case was not too long because it felt heavy in this home. I was solo, no team. I learned later that going alone was not a good idea. There was a lot going on and having some help would have made it easier to document what was happening and address the issues in this home. I just did what I needed to. I trusted and communicated with spirit. I was amazed at how much a cassette tape would pick up. It was only after I left and listened to the tape that I realized I had heard voices on the other side. I was shocked. I was up half the night with goosebumps. I shared my findings with the homeowner, and two weeks later she moved out and put the house up for sale.

I caught up with her several months later and she told me that the fire department was called one night because she thought her home was on fire. She smelled smoke everywhere, but no fire was found. That was the last straw for her. Sometime after that she learned that the past homeowner was a heavy smoker and had died in his bed with a burned-out cigarette in his hand. It could have burned down the house. The fire department had been called once before by a neighbor, when he was still alive, who thought they saw smoke coming from the house. For me that was a spiritual warning, because they found him. That year he passed in the home. Spirits have a way of intervening to protect us from things we cannot see, or before something happens.

There are aspects of the paranormal that seem to tie back to spiritual beliefs. I knew that if I wanted to continue to grow, I had to educate myself and understand all sides of this. I studied for years. I read all kinds of books and just dove into it. I felt that there had to be more than what I was being told. Before I knew it, I was being called again to a home where things just did not seem right. Back then equipment was limited. So, I just trusted my cassette player to help me hear whatever evidence appeared. Once the word got out, more and more cases started to come my way, and they continue until this day.

IT SEEMS LIKE THE QUIETER YOU BECOME
THE MORE YOU HEAR.
IN THE SILENCE SPIRIT SPEAKS TO YOU

Chapter 2

Fort Lauderdale, Florida

I got a call from a friend of mine in Fort Lauderdale about some strange things that had been going on at her home. For privacy reasons she will be referred to as "Lynn." My friend didn't go into many details, but I had a feeling she knew more than what she was telling me. I agreed to go visit. When I got to the house, the first thing that hit me was a bad smell. They had a party a few nights prior, so the house was kind of trashed so to speak. I just figured maybe they forgot to take out the garbage. Of course, her parents were out of town.

As I walked through the house and looked around, I finally met with Lynn and she started to tell me what was going on within the home: lights flickering, seeing shadows, and other noises she could not explain. When I inquired about the smell, she just looked at me. I asked, "Did anyone take out the trash?" She went on to say, "It's been like this the past few weeks."

I felt sick to my stomach. It was more than the usual, so I told her I would be back. I needed her to pick up and make it easier for me to actually walk and sit. She agreed. I decided to do some in-depth research. I knew about rancid odors, but I was not willing to go there just yet. I was still hoping it was just the trash needing to go out.

I figured it couldn't hurt to talk to the priest at the church we went to, Father Maurice. I will never forget the words he said to me. He said, "You do understand where there is good, there is also evil?" I looked at him and replied "Yes, I do, Father." Those words resonate with me to this day.

A week after that I went back to Lynn's house. I brought my cassette player. When I got to the house it was clean. There were candles burning, so I asked Lynn if she was ready to sit down and talk about everything going on in her home. I had a pen and paper for notes and my cassette recorder. I turned on the cassette recorder and started the session. I was still a one-person investigator at the time. As she started to talk, I noticed the lights flickering a few times. She said, "That's normal, it happens every so often."

We continued our conversation. For some reason I asked, "Can we blow out the candles?" I no sooner said that when the rancid odor came back. I told her, "It smells like something is dead. Did you take out the trash?" She responded, "Yes, the trash can is empty." I started to feel sick again, but this time I stayed.

The recorder kept going as I asked a bunch of questions, and finally the sixty-minute tape stopped. It got unusually cold in the room. Lynn got scared and said she needed to leave, I agreed. When I left, I listened to the tape. There was a lot of static and then I heard "Get out!" I played it over and over again and shared it with a friend. My friend told me it was crazy; it scared her.

I finally set up a meeting with Lynn at a place that we could talk outside of the house. I played the tape for her, and she flipped out. I needed to get more out of her, but she was scared. I just came out and asked, "Have you used a Ouija board?" She looked at me and admitted to using one the night of the party. It took weeks to deal with this. She got rid of the Ouija board, but the house was not the same. It never really cleared out, even after saging. I suggested having her home blessed.

Her parents came back from their trip to Europe, and two weeks after that her father committed suicide. Nothing was ever normal in that house again. I could not tell Father Maurice just yet; I was pretty upset over what happened. The church will not step in without a lot of proof and documentation. All I had to go on was a rancid odor, a Ouija board, and a suicide. When I finally spoke to Father Maurice, he prayed with me and blessed me for protection. I told him about the tape, but when I went to play it again the voice was gone. The tape had no static on it anymore. I was pretty sure that whatever it was had been tied to something evil and demonic in nature; you could just feel it.

I asked Lynn to never use a Ouija board again and she said she wouldn't. Two years later I heard she was in a car crash and did not survive. I never felt the same. Things changed for me from that day forward. I felt uneasy for months following that case. I was upset when I heard about Lynn's dad, and then two years later to hear of her death.

Whatever really happened in that house I may never know. It was powerful enough to punch a hole into this universe. I feel like it had influence over this family. Do I blame the Ouija board? I am not sure. What I am sure of is its presence and use in that home the night of the party. It was just too much. Much later I heard that people were saying the house was haunted. I know what I heard and know what I felt. It left me wondering for years.

Chapter 3

The Seven Signs of a Haunting

Before we go any further, it's important to know and understand the seven signs of a haunting.

They include, but are not limited to:
1. Unexplained physical injuries
2. Temperature changes
3. Objects moving
4. Unknown smell
5. Doors slamming
6. Items disappearing and reappearing
7. Strange shadows

These things can shake people up and make a true nonbeliever into a believer real fast. As a paranormal investigator I have seen things fly across a room, books come off shelves, and cameras going airborne from secure locations. Let's not forget those shadow figures that wake you at night; these are clear signs you have a haunting.

From the moment I had my first encounter with spirits at a young age I knew this would always be a part of my life. It may sound crazy, but I really enjoy speaking with spirits, and most of the time they are kind enough to talk to me.

Knowing the boundaries are important because sometimes you can identify a spirit as one that means no harm but has other intentions. It's been my experience that energy lingers. When you have a traumatic death it can contribute to residual energy left over, such as attachments to homes and possessions.

Energy can use many ways to enter the physical world, including portals, such as mirrors. If you notice some of the signs that I mentioned here, don't assume that it's just your imagination. Identifying and being certain of your claim is important, but don't be afraid to have someone investigate. I always ask clients seeking my help to try and get photos and videos when possible.

Giving someone peace is the key, and helping spirits cross over is gratifying, no doubt. Each case is unique and different, some have an explanation, and some don't. Either way, I feel it's my job to find out and assist when I can. Showing compassion, both to the living and to those who have passed on, is important to me. Always be on your guard in the event it's something more than a loved one trying to connect.

Chapter 4

Loxahatchee, Florida

My next case was in Loxahatchee, Florida, a place I called home for close to nine years. I knew that things had already happened in this small community. The town was on the verge of a major population burst. It was also a major dumping ground. Yes, a dumping ground. After doing some research, talking to locals, even digging up old news stories, it was evident that the area was a place to not only dump trash, but bodies. If a crime took place back in the day this area was rural and remote as hell, so it was a common place to dispose of bodies. Like I said, I did my own research. Now, is that enough to cause hauntings? Not necessarily, but I think that dying a traumatic death can contribute to the type of things that we will discuss in this next story.

One day I got a call from a family member. Her neighbors were having a lot of strange things going on that they simply could not explain. They had two small children and two dogs.

It was a small home tucked in a normal looking neighborhood. Things were getting crazy in this home, from the kids not sleeping, to the dogs acting weird, things moving, and lights going on and off. It got to the point that they just could not deal with it anymore. My kids were young and they went with me on what was supposed to be only a house blessing.

When I got there the house felt heavy. The husband was anxious to get it all to stop, so he took me room to room. Like I said, it was a small home. We started in the master bedroom, a place where it was especially active. The ceiling fan was on. No sooner had I walked into the room than the lights started flashing and the room temperature went down. He just looked at me and said, "This is what I am talking about." I knew it would be more than a house blessing.

I decided to go in a different direction with this and save the blessing for the end. I lit a candle and I started to walk the home. At the time I only had a Blackberry phone and cassette recorder on me, so not much in hand. After I walked out of the room I asked the family a lot of questions.

I was told there was a lot of activity at the end of the hall, the last room on the right that no one would sleep in anymore. It always felt cold. Their child heard unexplained noises. It was generally uncomfortable. They had hung a beautiful portrait of Jesus in the hall between the two rooms with lit candles. They said they put it there for protection.

I began to check all the rooms. The one on the right was colder, no doubt, and dark. As I made my way out of the room, I noticed the dog had followed me and was suddenly in front of me. He started to growl at me and backed me out one step at a time. He was drooling. My kids were freaking out, as

13

I had my back to everyone. I moved slowly. No one could get the dog to stop, he kept coming at me. I thought he was going to attack me. I got to the living room and we were eye to eye, me and this dog. All of a sudden the front door that was open, because I had saged earlier, slammed shut on its own and the dog just fell to the floor and started to whimper. I was so relieved. I was sure he was going to attack me. The home-owners freaked out.

I found out that they had gone to a flea market and picked up an old chair and some other things. I do believe in attach-ments. Was it a possibility? I don't know. Anything is possi-ble. Either way, they put the chair outside and never brought it back into the house. Things seemed to have calmed down for about two weeks. I was asked to return because the activity started up again. Lights were flashing, knocking sounds, and a growling dog. I walked the house to see if I could feel anything or pick up on anything. You could feel the heaviness. I was pretty sure it was attached to something in the home. The chair was still outside the house, and even though Ron and his wife loved flea market finds and antiquing, they stayed away after the first occurrence. It was a few months back and forth to this home, and with no relief in sight, the family moved.

It's always been my way of thinking that not everything comes with a clear answer. Some things can't be fixed that easily, and this was one of those situations.

So many cases like this would follow as I dug deeper into this mysterious world of the paranormal. I never imagined how far it would all go in the years to come.

Chapter 5

Tallahassee, Florida

Around 2012 I was called out to investigate a case at a college dorm. Here is how it all went down: Tallahassee, Florida, FSU off campus dorm apartments. It was pouring down rain. I had no idea what I was walking into. It all seemed normal looking on the outside. I made my way to the door and I was shocked to see five young girls. I thought maybe two, *but five?* The place was huge. They were so happy to see me, and relieved, like a weight was lifted. They were all so scared; you could see it in their faces.

I sat down to get to know them all a little better. We started talking to keep things normal. I asked them where they were all from and they quickly responded: Ft. Lauderdale, Broward County, and Miami. I was thrilled to hear they were all from my hometown area. We talked for quite a while. I mean, I had to calm the atmosphere and get them to focus on what I needed to know to help them. Once we started, there was no turning back.

I had a few people with me as that was the beginning of my team. The girls started telling me bits and pieces of what was going on. They had lights flashing and doors closing. It was some crazy stuff, but I felt something was being left out of this. Something they didn't want to tell me. I understood they were all scared, and rightfully so. It's all tied back to a hand-made Ouija board. The girls claimed the activity started after they had used it the weekend before I arrived. Was it the board or something else?

It was more than just the board; they had gone to a party and gotten deep into other things. One of the girls told me she had never felt this scared. As I said earlier, I do believe in attachments. I also believe that when you open a door, you better be prepared to deal with what may come through. After we talked and got everyone calmed down, we went ahead and took pictures and used a voice recorder. We caught a lot of things that I just couldn't brush off as nothing. There was an image in one of the photos that could not be explained, it looked like a shadow figure. We also photographed an orb. There were some strange sounds from areas of the apartment.

Once we completed the investigation we closed with a prayer and blessing. We saged the dorm and made sure that the handmade Ouija board was gone. They had dabbled in things they simply didn't understand but promised not to do it again. The girls stayed in touch, and about six months later graduated. Their time at FSU was done and they headed back to their roots in South Florida. As for the dorm, it's unclear if anything ever happened there again.

There were many claims from other students that came

forward about the FSU dorms, both on and off campus, having strange phenomena. After having activity in the dorms and around campus for some time, it has been said by many that have gone to school there that the FSU campus is haunted. Could it be tied to all the history near the school? The next story will shed some light on some of the history in Tallahassee.

The Old City Cemetery is not far. It was established in 1829 making it the oldest cemetery in Tallahassee. I did a walk-through of that location because I wanted to see the grave of the witch buried there known as Elizabeth "Bessie" Budd-Graham. The historic headstone is said to be the final resting place of the White Witch. Elizabeth Budd-Graham, Bessie, was only 23 years old when she died, leaving behind two small children and a husband. The legend about Bessie being a witch is due to a a number of unusual things about her grave. Although this cemetery is also the final resting place of many well-known people, including governors, her grave is the most visited.

Much has been said about this location close to college town, and there are many stories of the cemetery itself. Let's not forget Ted Bundy who walked the streets of Tallahassee on a murder rampage. I think it's safe to say that this college town has its own share of paranormal activity. It is one of the hot spots and the most visited by myself, and now my team. It's also the location of Native American Indian burial grounds.

Denise Burroughs

WHEN LAND IS DISTURBED
THAT'S WHEN THE DEAD WAKE UP AND
WE HEAR THEM

Living in North Florida has provided so many opportunities to explore the paranormal. I mean, the entire state of Florida has tons of history. There is much to be said of its past and what role that plays in what we call paranormal activity. It's not just limited to things that you think may have created energy, but it's tied directly to the location and the land. It's those hauntings that will likely never end no matter what you do. Tallahassee and its surrounding counties are perfect examples of this kind of phenomena.

In the pages to follow I will share more cases with you from Georgia to Florida. All the experiences I have shared so far led me to a full paranormal team and the creation of Paranormal Investigators of North Florida. After years of doing investigations alone I was ready for the next step, a full team to go with me to investigate some of the most haunted locations anywhere. Some are right here in our own backyard! In our towns and neighborhoods Paranormal Investigators of North Florida was born, and the rest is history.

The next chapter brought everything full circle. My cases have allowed me to further my ability and to communicate with spirits on many different channels, from a haunted house to an old building and more.

Denise Burroughs

THE COOL THING ABOUT WORKING
WITH SPIRIT IS IT SPEAKS.
VIBRATION IS ENERGY

Resting place Elizabeth Budd-Graham

Chapter 6

Georgia

Not every ghost experience is scary, believe it or not. Not all are because of rituals or objects. How is that possible? It just happens. Every case and situation is different and I think it's important to shed a little light on that.

Sometimes spirits come as a warning, not to hurt or scare. One of my cases in Georgia was one of those situations. The home felt uneasy for the homeowners on and off as things started to happen. They were having trouble sleeping. There were cold spots and lights going on and off, mostly in the late hours of the night. The family had a child and they were afraid for her. When I got the call, it was clear that we needed to go because a child was in the home. That's all I needed to know. We drove almost two hours to get to them.

When we arrived, it was dark. It was a mobile home in an older neighborhood; it just had a vibe to it as we pulled up.

When we entered, the place was cold and half lived in. I didn't feel like it was evil or anything, just off.

We set up and did a general interview with the couple that lived here. They were concerned about their daughter and her *imaginary playmate*. There was an infestation of roaches that could not be explained. The house was clean and the cause was unknown. We did room checks while we were setting up and it became clear we were not alone. It started to feel heavy. The equipment went off within seconds. One of my team members felt uneasy and had to stop. She said that she couldn't breathe.

I walked out to see what was going on, and before she could tell me anything, I turned around and saw an image of a fire in my mind. I could see the house, I could see the fire. It was fast. I didn't say anything. I walked over to her, and she said, "I smelled smoke, I couldn't breathe." Ditto, it confirmed the vision that I had moments before. We went back in and continued to investigate. It was about an hour later that the homeowners told me that a fire took place in the home. It was an electrical fire.

After spending several hours with the family, I felt that whatever was there was trying to warn them. The family moved out four months later. Several months after they moved, another fire broke out and the house was a total loss. It's cases like this that I feel instead of it being something bad, it happens as a warning.

The spirit's energy may have saved their lives. This is what I call a spiritual warning. One thing I will say is that having as much information as possible going into cases is important. We do a lot of research and try to find out as much as we can on most of the locations before we arrive.

Some, on the other hand, don't have any historical records. They don't go all the way back, or there just simply is not enough information on hand. A lot of times records are burned. Many have been lost in a fire and dates do not match up. Knowing as much as you can find out helps a lot. On those cases where you can't get enough information, you just do your best because history is the key.

Chapter 7

Lake Jackson, Florida

There is so much to be said about this case. I have visited this home several times over the last couple of years. This location is close to a Native American Burial Ground. It seemed like it wasn't just my client having issues, but the entire neighborhood. This was all vacant land at one time, and a huge amount of this land was part of the Native Burial Grounds.

In addition to my client, there was a local minister that stated he heard voices in his home and saw shadow figures. One night he felt a strong presence in the home, and he said he knew it wasn't God. The neighbors were hearing noises, seeing shadows, unexplained flickering of lights, and generally there was just a heavy feeling. They reported these things to my client but did not want to come forward at the time. I believe they were afraid of seeming crazy.

Long story short, this land was cleared and whatever was

buried in the dirt was distributed throughout the neighborhood. Was this the reason why so many were having problems in later years? It's a distinct possibility as to why some of the homeowners have reported unexplained things going on in their homes.

To this day there is still a lot going on in the home that was the subject of our investigation. The home itself seems to have an active portal entry and tons of spirit energy crossing through it.

Spirit box sessions gave names and dates and even spoke about previous homeowners. They also identified a Tribal Chief and burial where the home sits. Let's not forget, it's less than three miles from the Native American Burial Mounds site.

We returned to this home a year later to check in and there was still a lot of paranormal activity. We will continue to investigate here to try and figure out a way to keep the homeowners and the spirit energy on even ground. The homeowners don't want to move, and I doubt the energy will ever fully go away. Sometimes people can live with whatever is going on, and at times they can't. Only time will tell with this case.

Burial sites are sacred and should be treated as such, the deceased desire that respect. You know that old saying "When in a cemetery don't step on a grave," there is a reason for that. If you're going to move a grave site *move everything*, not just the headstone.

Native American Burial Mounds are usually marked, but not in all cases. Those burial sites are usually raised graves and not too hard to identify. Playing it safe in those locations that are prone to be a place of burial is important, regardless of the situation or location.

Lake Jackson House

Denise Burroughs

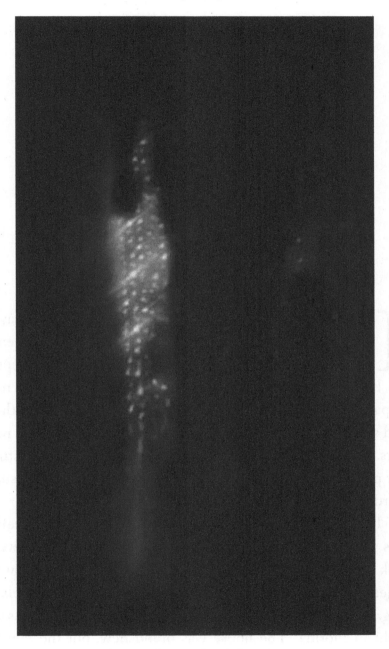

Laser grid image of spirit formation

Chapter 8

Mallard Trace, Florida

I could not even imagine what was to come on the day I got this call. The shaky, unsure voice on the other end of the phone was looking for answers. She was skeptical, but she told me it was her last shot. She stated she had not unpacked her belongings and found a box in the home that had some items, such as a few furnishing pieces that were not hers. Shortly after she started rummaging through the stuff her personality started to change. She started writing unusual words on the bathroom mirror in an unknown language.

I took the case, but I could not imagine how bad it really was going to be. The moment we pulled up, before we even took our equipment out of the car, the air felt so thick. It was quiet for a Florida summer night. Not a sound, not even a frog. That was unusual, you always hear frogs or crickets at night in Florida. The house was brand new, but the family was clearly having a hard time.

I noticed there were mirrors everywhere, I counted at

least six, and they were in every room. My team members set up like we always do, and within five minutes our batteries went dead. We had to reload all the equipment. Most of the evidence was visible to the naked eye, it was crazy.

We saw a dark shadow figure walking towards two of my team members. All we could do was to tell them to run. We got some incredible pictures of this figure as well. As we were doing a session in the living room, figures were stepping out of one of the mirrors. There were animals and Native Americans, they were all moving to the mirror to get out. There was this one large figure that stepped out and moved towards the front door to go out. It must have passed close to one of my team members because he became sick. A short time later this figure regained entry back into the house and reentered the mirror. We got a voice recording telling us to "Get out."

The homeowner was in a lot of distress. She came out of her room, and about ten minutes later a mark appeared on her neck. It was bright red and in a place that she could not have reached herself, not to mention there were cameras running all through the house.

It was one of the craziest, yet eeriest cases we have ever been on. Everyone was uneasy in this house. As we were leaving, a team member took one last photo. A while later after looking at the photo we all noticed a hand coming out of the mirror. We still have that picture. It was insane.

Shortly after we left, within the week, the family left the house with only the clothes they had, never to return. We do know that one mirror was removed from the home, but I can't say for sure whether it stayed out of the home or not after we left.

The family was worried that no one would believe them. I'll never forget what was said to me when I took this case. I asked if there were any pictures that I could see. The reply was "You will see it with your own eyes," and we did! The evidence showed itself. I never heard from this family again. I never went back to that neighborhood. However, I know that the home has sold three or more times since they left.

Hand coming out of the mirror

Chapter 9

Greystone Manor

The Greystone Manor was built in 1904 by a merchant and hotel owner named Thomas Faulkner. It became a hotel in 1918, and an apartment building years later. It is rumored that at some point it was used to store bodies when the funeral home across the street ran out of space. Today it has been restored to a private residence. The records in this town are scarce to say the least, but there are plenty of stories about Greystone Manor.

Before the Greystone was built, this property is said to have been the site of a wooden rooming house that was home to ten orphaned children that were placed there in the care of a local tobacco farmer after the death of their parents. Local lore says that the children were forced to work the tobacco fields and that the farmer was abusive, especially targeting the two oldest girls. One night when he was too drunk to catch them, the children locked themselves in their room. They slammed the door causing a kerosene lamp to fall off the mantle and break, which started a fire that burned the house to the ground killing everyone inside.

My first paranormal encounter at the Greystone was in the mid-2000s when the homeowner was having a haunted house during Halloween. My daughter, who was already living in Perry, invited me to go. I went and it was fun, but my natural radar as I call it was already on.

I could feel so much energy coming from this house. As I was entering the porch area, I felt like we were all being watched, and I believe we were. As I was leaving the home I walked down a sidewalk to go to my car and I turned my head and saw a man, a woman, and two children standing on the back steps. The woman was in a white dress, and she had short hair. Her children were in knee-length shorts with suspenders and long-sleeve shirts. The father was wearing what looked to be a coat with tails, he was tall. The mother had her hands on the children's shoulders who were standing in front of her. They just stared at me.

I stopped and looked at my daughter. I said, "Do you see them?" She replied, "See who?" I pointed. She said, "No, but I believe you see them." I couldn't take my eyes off them. My daughter called

my name and said, "Mom." I turned my head and when I looked back they were gone. I often pass that side street and I look all the time to see if they are there.

After moving to this town some years later I had the opportunity to do a paranormal investigation at the Greystone. We spent three and a half hours there and our equipment picked up a lot of energy. We saw shadow formations of faces, and it was especially active on the second and third floors. During our investigation of the third floor, we noticed small fingerprints appearing on what looked to be charred beams. As fast as they appeared, they disappeared. We were able to get pictures of this. One of the spirits in the house is that of a child who responds to the name, Sarah. Many have reported seeing Sarah, and we did find information about a child by that name with a connection to the house.

There is a lady in the tower that has been seen by many locals, including myself. Many have seen her and taken photos of the apparition of a woman in white in the tower. I lived in a property adjacent to the Greystone and my husband and I have observed the figure in the tower windows. Some people say that she is the spirit of a woman that was stabbed to death in the bathtub. I think of her as the lady of the house, but we don't really know who she is. Although records are scarce, there is no doubt this home is active.

In early 2019 I was interviewed for a magazine. During that conversation I told my story about the family that I saw on the back steps at Greystone Manor. John, the journalist for Greene Publishing interviewing me, looked at me and said, "I have seen them too." I was shocked that someone else saw the same apparitions that I saw. John and I have spoken many times since then because I have been featured in the magazine *The Front Porch* twice. A photo for the magazine was taken on the front porch of the Greystone.

Today the Greystone Manor is lived in, however I am pretty sure it still has guests roaming the upstairs halls in this beautiful fourteen-room mansion. The history here continues. It's a staple in this small town and always will be. History is everywhere and everything tells us a story, even a haunting. One thing is for sure, the old buildings in small towns have some of the best cases I have investigated.

Greystone Manor

Denise Burroughs

Appearing and disappearing fingerprints on charred beam

Denise Burroughs

Charred beam on third floor

Denise Burroughs

Greystone bathtub

Denise Burroughs

Greystone tower where the lady in white is often seen

Chapter 10

The Cemetery

A place of rest. How could there be anything else, right? That is what we are led to believe, but not in this particular cemetery. For the privacy of the location and respect for the families who are laid to rest here, we will just say this cemetery is located in Florida in a quiet little town outside of the city. I'd heard many stories about things that had already happened here, but I had to visit to believe it. It hits you all at once as soon as you step into the location.

One evening I went out to this cemetery. I was with some of my team members and we were investigating claims of negative energy. It was a cold January night; you could see your breath. We felt frozen. I had been told to stay away from the right side of the cemetery, that something dark was there. The group and I set up in the middle of the cemetery. It felt so off that we made a circle with our backs to each other facing out. We felt we needed to see what otherwise would be behind us. The equipment that night was way off. It was too cold. There were moments of just freezing.

There was a grave there, like a child's headstone, dating back to the early 1800s. I am pretty sure none of the family would still be alive. I mention this grave because it was a site of rituals, spirit board sessions, candles and beads. It was a sad and odd scene that this grave was a haven for this stuff. There had to be a reason why. Oddly though, this grave sat close to the right side of the cemetery, close to the side we were told to stay away from.

This place gets so creepy at night that local police officers have reported feeling odd sensations in the cemetery. When we got there we heard growling sounds. We felt our hair standing up on end. You felt like you were not alone. However, the lights — I just can't explain those lights coming right towards us. They looked like the bright lights from a four-wheeler, but no one was there. They were moving fast and coming straight on. We started to get nervous as they came towards us but they just disappeared. There is a fence so no vehicle of any kind could be there. This could not be mistaken for flashlights. We plan to return to this location again. Something about this experience just makes you want to go back.

I think it's important to say that although I mention the spirit board, Ouija by name, I don't have anything against them. They are tools, no different than a spirit box. When it comes to a Ouija board I believe in "hello" and "goodbye." It's important to close a session, many don't. I think that when you open a door things can happen, and they usually do. You need to understand what you are doing. It's not something I use during my cases, but I know many have different thoughts about this. I am neutral but have done cases that have gone horribly wrong before we get there because of things that are done — and done wrong.

Everything you do should always be done with thought and care. You don't want to open a door that you can't close. That's when nightmares begin.

Child's grave in the cemetery

Chapter 11

Rosewood

I have investigated so many places over the years, but one that really stood out to me was Rosewood. This was the scene of a racially motivated massacre in 1923 where over 30 people were killed and the town was burned to the ground. And although only one home remains, the energy here can still be felt.

There are a lot of reports of paranormal activity in this area. One of the most popular stories surrounding Rosewood is about a ghostly black man that is said to protect innocent people who venture into the woods. Others have claimed to have heard gunshots and loud screams coming from the woods at all hours of the night.

Rosewood is located just off State Road 24, fourteen miles northeast of Cedar Key. We were traveling in this area and decided to stop. Rosewood was settled in the year 1845, and the only home still standing is the home of John Wright, the landmark of Rosewood. It has changed hands many times through the years. When my team and I visited this location, we stood on the side of the road. You could feel the energy here. We were able to stand by the road and the road's edge with plenty of room, thankfully, as there was still a lot of traffic on the busy highway. Not needing to go any further, and using equipment, we got a ton of responses to questions we asked and some incredible pictures.

Not everyone believes in orbs, but I do. There simply was no other way to describe the colorful glow and rainbow effect we saw, even with the naked eye. One stood face to face with the camera. Knowing the history of this location, I really had no doubt about what I saw or felt that night. It was so real and intense. That orb was captured on camera. It was amazing.

It was a long trip to visit this location, we drove 100 miles to be exact. We plan to visit again soon. There are just so many stories about Rosewood. There is speculation as to whether or not the last standing home built in 1923 will become a museum. The events of this era were tragic; the loss of life here was horrific. It was a terrible time in history, but the land is alive. The souls of those lost here, I believe, are still present at times wanting to be acknowledged.

Orb

Denise Burroughs

Orbs

Chapter 12

Cassadaga

In my travels through Florida another location that really hits home is Cassadaga. It's a spiritual community that goes back to 1875, founded by a trance medium named George P. Colby from Pike, NY. If you're gifted in any way, this place is for you. Even if you're not gifted spiritually, the energy here will impact you regardless.

I was drawn here and visited many times. One of the reasons I went to Cassadaga was to visit Lake Helen-Cassadaga Cemetery and the location of the Devil's Chair. The gravestones date back to the early 1800s. The whole place had an odd vibe to it, I am talking about the cemetery. Colby, the founder of Cassadaga, is buried here and his spirit is one of several that have been seen wandering the grounds. I went there to see the Devil's Chair, but did not get too close, nor did I sit in the chair.

So, what happens here? According to one local legend, an unopened can of beer left on the chair will be empty by morning. In some accounts, the can is opened, and in others, the beer is simply gone through the unopened top. Many say that the Devil himself speaks to you when you sit in the chair, and some report hearing voices in their head when seated. Others say the Devil outright appears to those who sit in the chair. People report having bad luck after sitting in the chair or getting sick afterward. Me being extremely sensitive, I felt uneasy here and had no desire to sit in the chair. I felt heavy and out of it for a while.

We were visiting with friends, and while in the cemetery my group kind of disappeared. I felt like I was in a tunnel. It was weird. However, I felt this strong urge to go closer to the chair. I did move closer and got lightheaded and felt sick for a minute. It was then that out of the corner of my eye a dark shadow darted past me. I heard shuffling sounds. It sounded like someone was running through the fall leaves, yet I was alone. I captured some pictures. I did see some orbs. When I found my friends and husband again, it was like they just reappeared. It was strange.

Without a doubt it was an odd experience. Many have felt the same way. It makes you wonder. I will definitely return to the "Psychic Capital of the World." It's truly my element and it feeds me so much positive energy when I am there. As far as the Devil's Chair, sure I will visit again, but I am not sure if I will ever want to sit in it. Something in the back of my mind tells me not to, at least for now.

My cases through the years have been all over Florida, the place I call home. In 2019 my team and I filmed a web series *called Haunted Florida*. You can watch it on YouTube. We had a great time filming at haunted locations and in homes. I would say without a doubt that this state is rich in history, both good and bad. It has some unsettling things that happen for many reasons, either the land, the home, or its location.

No doubt Florida has some of the most haunted locations and my team and I have been lucky enough to investigate a lot of them, from the southern tip of the state to the North Florida area.

Devil's Chair

Chapter 13

A Haunting on Wilcox

This is one of those investigations that goes against everything normal. It started as just a call to come out and investigate some strange things going on, especially impacting the dog in the home. The homeowner had started taking pictures of the dog and caught orbs flying around the house. The dog had more agitation than I have ever seen before when it comes to animals reacting to spirits. The dog was constantly spinning her head, crying and whining.

It was a Saturday night and we arrived around 7:30 p.m. When I first walked in, I felt like we were being mocked. It felt off, just a heaviness in the air. As time went on it became clear that much more could be happening here.

The furniture in the home that was there didn't belong to the homeowners, some was left behind and other pieces were secondhand. I started facing the hallway and decided to put the REM-POD on the floor. The REM-POD is a high sensitivity device that captures spirit energy from a wide area using colored lights and audible tones to alert when the energy field is disturbed. Just like that, in a few seconds it went off as if to say, *I am here*. I then realized we were in for an interesting night. However, it didn't end there.

This home sits in a neighborhood that has a violent history. In the past there was racial violence, including murder and lynchings. At least five families moved in and out of this house in a short period of time, no one ever stayed long. In more recent history a small child was injured and died as a result of her injuries. The homeowner believes that the ghost of this child resides in the home in what was her former bedroom.

Lights go on and off, the TV goes off by itself, and orbs are everywhere. The family dog was being tormented. The unusual effect it had on the dog could not be explained, even by the vet. In-home cameras captured large masses and shadow figures. The evidence caught on camera was hard to dispute.

The homeowner had been attending church on a regular basis and had the house blessed when she first moved in. Once the strange activity started she went to the Catholic church to see if they could help. An audio recording was caught that alarmed the homeowner as well as the church, "Fear the Prince." It was not your normal case at all.

I believe the final straw was when the client could not walk into the church without feeling ill. She mentioned having an irrational feeling of wanting to burn the church down and set the priest on fire as he was blessing the Eucharist. It was at that point I went to the Catholic church myself and we took all our documentation with us and had a meeting. The client and I were interviewed by the priest and asked to write our experiences separately. After he read both of our letters he was on board. The Catholic church had decided to get involved. This was a first for me.

It was a tedious process and the client was required to go through a counseling session to make sure she was mentally stable. She also received a number of Sacraments, such as, Confession and Anointing of the Sick. Many prayers were said, including prayers for protection. She was blessed with holy water and blessed oil. These rituals took about two to three hours. The house was then blessed again. It seemed to calm things down a little bit, but the activity started back up in the months ahead.

We kept the church in the loop as to what was going on. The local priest reached out to an exorcist who is well versed in demonology. You cannot exorcise a home or property, just a person, but they both came out to do a heavy blessing on the home and the land. The client was counseled again by the exorcist priest for about an hour. He explained what they were going to do and there were strict instructions the client had to follow. It started out with many prayers, then they began the process. The blessing was done in Latin and repeated in English, both priests wore special robes and sashes. This was the third blessing of the home. This was a really strong blessing. However, everything ramped back up just two weeks later.

The homeowner became uncomfortable with the situation and reached out to me again. The dog was even more agitated than before. One night the client was awakened around three in the morning by her dog's cry. She just assumed that the dog stepped on something or was having a nightmare. When the client awoke the next day the dog was cowering in a corner and had three distinct, deep scratches on her back about a foot from the tail. The vet said there was no way this dog could have done that herself. To this day the scars from those scratches are highly visible.

One afternoon she decided to clean out her SD cards from the master bedroom camera. As she was sifting through the photos, she stumbled onto one photo that left her speechless, terrified, and unsure of what to do. She contacted me and when I finally received the photo I was shocked by what I saw. It was a full body apparition hovering just inches over her while she slept. She sent the photo to the priest and the church did offer to return. In the meantime, we decided to try something else.

I set up another investigation, but this time to do a full evaluation. The last time we went out there we placed iron railroad spikes at all four corners of the home. Iron spikes are believed to bind spirit energy. They were placed there to protect by binding the energy. However, there may have been some energy already trapped in the home since the last time we were there.

I work closely with some team members who are spiritual, not religious, and they are all about natural elements of the earth. We had nothing to lose at this point, so we decided to perform a ritual that dates back a couple of hundred years. A ritual sword made of iron was placed on the bed in the room that was infested with spirit energy. The iron in the sword draws out, absorbs, and binds the negative energy in the same way that the iron spikes do. The sword is then taken out and driven into the ground to disperse the negative energy. A ceremony was done to release the energy from the railroad spikes and the sword to cleanse the home and land once again. This went on for several hours

The images we got from the camera in the master bedroom during this process were unreal. Black masses and shadows all over the room. The room was covered as we watched on a screen from another room.

Between the sage and other elements we used, it took what seemed like forever, but it slowly made its way out of the room and left through the window. We all watched as those dark energies exited one by one. They were fighting to stay. Eventually they all went out the window. We all smelled what was like bad cologne from the '70s. That odor masked the horrible smell of what reminded me of rotten eggs.

The room started to clear out. We were making good progress. The room fully cleared out after forty-five minutes, it stayed that way after a ton of sage, salt, and special blessings were done. I am hopeful that this is over with. We are hoping for the best as we move forward from this difficult case. I believe in using whatever means are available if it helps someone.

Soon after writing this story, I was notified that the spirit activity has returned. So, we will likely be back with the church on standby. We don't know why, but the home seems to become more active in the fall.

The homeowners continue to experience paranormal phenomena within the home and likely will for some time, regardless of what measures are taken. I do believe it's all tied to the land and the land's past, which will never go away. I believe that the veil is thin and that our world and the spirit realm are really close. I feel it's been thinning for some time. I have witnessed a lot of paranormal activity in the last few years, more than usual. Strong moon cycles, and bigger effects from it.

It's a process, a change in vibration. It's spirit speaking to all of us. Its frequency is just getting louder for more people to hear it, feel it, and actually see it.

Spirit formation hovering over homeowner

Denise Burroughs

Dog reacting to orbs

Denise Burroughs

Dog reacting to possible spirit energy

Chapter 14

Haunted Objects

When I got into paranormal research I acquired many things along the way. Some I've kept, others I've gotten rid of. I am referring to haunted objects. By no means am I a collector, but I have had many people give me objects or dolls that they simply feel have something tied to them. They are afraid to keep them in their homes.

A lot of people are afraid of clowns and dolls, they just don't like the way they look. I was never a fan of clowns, the only one I have is packed in a box. It was given to me by my grandmother, it's a childhood memento. As for dolls, I have only collected a few.

During this time in my life, any dolls or clowns I do get are special because they have some sort of attachment to them. Some of them are just a simple haunt, others not so much. Sometimes it's more.

I recently acquired one doll whose origins are unknown.

The woman who gave her to me stated that the doll was in her bedroom in one spot, and when she came back later the doll was on her bed. Cameras in the home captured the doll moving by itself. Her eyes were also witnessed moving.

Since not much was known about the doll, it made me wonder if I should be truly concerned about her once she was in my possession. I decided to be cautious with her. I named her within a few days of having her. I named her Phoenix. It simply means *reborn,* living through life cycles. I still have no real history on this doll as she is.

I took her in and tested the waters to see if anything would happen. She has been active on camera. I have seen her eyes move and her cheeks get red, and no doubt she does react when spoken to. During an EVP session, she responded to questions by turning a flashlight on and off multiple times. During spirit box sessions she claims that she is the devil. She is inhabited by a male spirit and her voice comes across as male on the spirit box. I simply don't know enough about her, so she is safely kept in a case to be viewed and not touched.

I never thought I would ever collect anything haunted. Somehow, I have become the doll keeper. There is a bail bonds office next to my paranormal office and people have dropped little haunts off for me to pick up — at a bail bonds office of all places. I don't mind taking them in as long as they all behave, that's how I deal with them. I was once given a haunted windup music box that would go off and on by itself. I no longer have that.

I tell people all the time, it's no different than anything you may bring home. You can bring anything home with you, even from a client's home when they call for help. From dolls to flea market items, you never know what you're going to get. These are called attachments. I believe in cleansing things. I use sage a lot and it works to clear the space and any energy. I am all about crystals and good energy.

I think it's safe to say that not every investigation is haunted. I can say that, if nothing more, I have met some great people along the way. If I had to give any advice to a new paranormal investigator I would say enjoy what you do, always be kind to your clients, and understand their journey. If you land on a true haunted location, always respect the situation and be cautious in what you do.

Denise with spirit board

Denise Burroughs

Haunted doll Phoenix

Denise Burroughs

Haunted dolls Sunshine and Eloise

Chapter 15

Cross City, Florida

I did an investigation at an old restaurant in Cross City. This place had been serving for years. Many say they have seen and felt strange things while dining here. I have to agree. The bathroom is a spot where you never feel alone. People are hesitant to go into this bathroom, there's just a feeling like you are being watched.

During an investigation, we did pick up a lot of activity on the K2

meters and some videos of shadows moving throughout the building. Located in the dining area and near the freezer, many staff have witnessed things in the kitchen after closing. Things were often misplaced, or dishes just fell off the counters. No one liked to stay there alone at night and they could not wait to leave.

As I was walking through the building I had several doors just slam shut, then another would open. It was crazy. It has been said that back in the day they used the freezer for storing bodies of those who had passed during the Seminole Wars.

Patrons have seen what seems to be a man wearing a cowboy hat just standing in a corner. As for the bathroom, it is uncomfortable and you get an uneasy feeling going in. Things still move around late at night. The activity continues to this day; in the kitchen the plates still fall and things get misplaced. It's clear, based on conversations with the staff, that no one likes to stay there at night. When it's time to go, it's time to go. There was a server who was left alone one night to close. She clearly stated she heard a bunch of commotion in the kitchen. It scared her enough to make her run out as quickly as she could, locking the door behind her. There is no doubt the history and its past still linger here today.

Across the street stands the Putnam Hotel, it's also been rumored to have guests report strange happenings in the upstairs rooms. Native Americans traveled through the area. There is also a secret room located in this hotel. We didn't get to see it because they keep it blocked and unused. The Putnam has a steak house and great dining, as well as the friendly spirits. People I have interviewed that have stayed there experienced the paranormal, but never felt as if it was anything too negative. I am sure you can stay in one of the rooms there that have been said to be haunted.

The restaurant and the hotel both had their share of activity. Walking around the Putnam property we picked up a lot on the K2 meters and the REM-POD. We gathered a lot of evidence from these places.

This entire area was traveled heavily back in the day. A lot is left here. Although it has been updated, it goes way back in time. The history alone explains a lot. There are visitors who still wander these locations to this day.

Spirit in window Cross City Restaurant

Denise Burroughs

Freezer once used for bodies

Chapter 16

Myths and Legend: UFOs and Bigfoot

UFOs have been recorded throughout human history, the only thing that's changed is how we interpret these events. Some early sightings may have been natural occurrences that our ancient ancestors didn't understand, like comets or asteroids, but others still have no modern explanations. In ancient times there was a tendency to attribute unexplained things in the sky as something religious. By the 19th and 20th century people began to interpret these things in the sky as technological. Reported UFO sightings exploded during World War II and continue to this day.

I have studied unidentified flying objects to some extent, but I am not an expert. Between 1948 and 1969 there were more than 12,000 reported UFOs. My personal UFO encounter came when I was on a visit to New Mexico. I spent some time out in the desert in an area where there have been many claims of UFO sightings. I stayed out one evening and saw something in the night sky that I can't explain. It didn't look like a star to me. Could it have been something more? I don't know, but it is possible.

Bigfoot, also known as Sasquatch, is often described as a large, hairy creature that walks on two legs like a human. Bigfoot is said to have a muscular build and stands seven to ten feet tall and is typically described as brown or dark in color. Bigfoot is said to reside in forests and wilderness areas.

Many Native Tribes say that Bigfoot has shapeshifting abilities and believe that they can transform into other animals or even humans at will. The Lummi tell stories of it appearing as a deer or a bear to trick hunters, only to reveal their true form when shot with an arrow. The Nootka of Vancouver Island believe that Sasquatch can turn invisible or teleport from one place to another. Still other tribes see Bigfoot as an interdimensional being that moves between the physical world and the spirit realm.

The name Sasquatch is believed to come from the word Sasq'ets, used by the Chehalis, meaning "wild man" or "hairy man." Sasquatch has a history going back many thousands of years in the oral stories of the Sts'ailes people from the Chehalis Lakes region of British Columbia. Sasquatch is an important part of their cultural and spiritual beliefs. Their ancestors tell a story of how Sasquatch is a caretaker who watches over the land. The Sts'ailes people claim a close bond with Sasquatch, and believe it has the ability to move between the physical and spiritual realm at will.

In Florida we have what is known as the Skunk Ape. This creature is described the same as Bigfoot with the only notable difference being the color of its hair or fur being described as reddish-brown in color. Growing up in Florida I heard about sightings all the time, especially in the Everglades. One of the earliest reported sightings was in 1942 when a man in Suwanee County reported this creature rushing out from the brush line while he was driving down an isolated road. It was said to have grabbed onto his vehicle and beat on the running board and door for half a mile before running away.

I know many who have spent a lot of hours hunting and researching Bigfoot. I am sure I know a lot less about Bigfoot than most. The same goes for UFOs. I leave nothing off the table and I am intrigued by both.

Chapter 17

Monticello, Florida

Monticello, Florida was incorporated in 1831. Monticello is home to the Letchworth-Love Burial Mounds. There are a ton of historical buildings and homes, which include an opera house and an old jail dating back to the Civil War. It has a rich history and is a town still connected to its past. This town is so magical and it's definitely filled with spirits. I have both visited and investigated the area.

One of the most well-known haunted locations in Monticello is the Old Jefferson County Jail. It was built in 1909 and used until sometime in the 1970s. The building underwent renovations in 1940 and again in 1960. This old brick building is now a historic site. You can feel a heaviness inside. The paint on the floors is chipped and peeling. There are white bricks in one area that have ominous notes scrawled on them by prisoners of long ago. There is a lot of death and misery tied to this location.

The Roseland Cemetery was founded soon after the end of the Second Seminole War at about the same time that the State of Florida was admitted into the union in 1845. The cemetery property was an expansion of the original 1827 City Cemetery. This location is known to have very active spirits. When I visited Roseland Cemetery I had equipment with me and the readings were off the charts.

Another well-known haunted location in Monticello is the Opera House. This historic theatre was built in 1890 by businessman John H. Perkins and was originally known as "The Perkins Block." The first floor of the building housed Perkins' general store, a sewing machine shop, and hardware store. The second floor was The Perkins Opera House. In 1972 it was restored as the Monticello Opera House and added to the National Register of Historic Places. Today it serves as a civic center for Jefferson County. It is believed to be haunted by John H. Perkins. There have been reports of multiple ghost sightings, including that of a figure that has been seen at the window of the ladies' dressing room. People also say that the lights turn on and off by themselves. It seems like an active location, although I have not yet done an investigation inside.

There are also a number of haunted residences in Monticello. Built in 1897, the Daffodale House is notorious for its haunts of a fascinating past — everything from strange music to aromas of pipe smoke that can be smelled when no one is smoking, to lights that go on and off, to the lady in white who roams the grounds at night. Many years ago, I went on a ghost tour there and brought a K2 meter and was able to pick up readings in and around the property itself. During my visit you could sense a spiritual presence on the grounds. It's not always active when you visit, but for the most part there is always something going on in the home. The most activity is said to be in the attic, it's definitely a great location.

Another historic home is the former residence of John Denham, a Scottish businessman. The Denham-Lacy house was built in 1872 and was added to the National Register of Historic Places in 1982. In addition to the ghost of John Denham, the home is rumored to be haunted by the friendly ghost of a former occupant, a schoolteacher named Sarah. The house is a bed and breakfast today.

There are many other haunted homes in the historic district and I recommend taking one of the haunted tours offered in Monticello. Many homes in this small town have a past, and many residents and visitors have seen the spirits that have been left behind. It's no wonder that this small, quaint town is known as one of the most haunted in the south.

Old Jail

Denise Burroughs

Monticello Opera House

Chapter 18

The Natural Bridge

This is a historical landmark located in Woodville, Florida just outside of Tallahassee. A lot of things take place here, such as Civil War reenactments, among other things.

Several years back I went out to this location on a hunch after first hearing about it. We were not exactly in the park, but just outside of it in the surrounding area. I honestly lost my sense of direction with all the heavily tree-lined and wooded areas. The leaves from the trees were starting to drop, as fall was upon us.

My team and I walked on an embankment. We got as close as we could to put our equipment on the ground, without it rolling down the small slope, just to see if anything would happen. It was cold that night, so we only stayed a few hours.

Many have said you can hear the sound of drums from Native Tribes that were once in the area. I really wanted to hear this if at all possible. I mean, this was an area that was heavily traveled by soldiers at war. There is a lot of history here to say the least.

We hung out on a small hill; nothing was happening. We were talking amongst ourselves when suddenly the K2 meter went off. I still didn't think much of it until someone else asked, *Is there anyone here?* The K2 meter went off once again, so we started to ask questions.

We decided to walk down this small hill and go a little further. The K2 meter went totally red and out of nowhere I heard the faint, surreal sound of a drumbeat. I didn't think too much about it then, *bam*, just like that the K2 meter went crazy. We were all amazed. For about 20 seconds we heard the sound of a drum beating.

I have to say it was one of the coolest experiences I ever had. I didn't believe any of this at first. I only went on a hunch like, *okay, I will check it out*, thinking not much would happen.

We wound up staying there for two hours. The K2 meter was responding to questions. Our recorder did capture the faint sound of the drum, but it was too low to share. I wish we had gotten a better recording of the drum. It was amazing. Many people say that the land still speaks. I do believe that. Every year there is a reenactment, it's like reliving the past with the cannons going off and all that they do for the display of history.

Some have said that you can see a green glow off the water on the lower hill where it fills with rainwater. It hardly ever dries out.

Honestly, all I saw was the moonlight shining through the trees. In the distance it was glowing off the water.

I have not gone back, it's been years. I may just have to revisit to see if once again we can hear the sound of the Native American drums.

It was an amazing experience for all of us that night.

EVERYONE'S STORY IS IMPORTANT. IMPORTANT ENOUGH TO LISTEN AND NOT WALK AWAY

Chapter 19

The Triangle Hauntings

T here is a reason this chapter gets this title, because there are three homes oddly involved. The backyard of this home is connected to two other homes. In 2019 I investigated a home that had a lot of strange events. The family themselves by no means lived in peace. The children hardly stayed at home, not even in their own rooms.

The daughter's room was constantly under attack from what appeared to be an old man. She claimed he stood at the foot of her bed, as crazy as it sounds. I believe children when they speak of such things. The things that were described to me a child would not know about, unless it actually happened. The closet in this room led to another location in the home. There was a hidden passage that went from the bedroom to the back of the kitchen. It was an eerie space. On video we clearly captured shadow figures moving in this room.

The family all smelled smoke one night and thought the

house was on fire. This family was totally under attack by something that no one had a clear understanding of, or where it came from. The only history we know of is a large fire at a gas plant. That fire and explosion happened in 1998. Based on research, although there were several injuries and loss of homes, there was no loss of life that we could confirm from that explosion and fire. Each of the homes, including the ones I am speaking of, all have had unexplained activity.

The family of this house lived in fear, and the homeowner worked from home when she could. That was difficult for her as the lights were constantly flashing on and off, there were burning smells, and the TV would go on and off by itself. She also noticed mood changes happening to herself. She became distant towards family and friends. We decided that after a few requests we would go out to the home.

The first thing I did was to set up the cameras. Now the homeowner did it as well, she wanted her daughter's room watched at all times. I can't blame her — the footage she got was truly unreal — evidence that something was there. Our equipment responded as well to all the questions, and even cut our equipment off, or drained the batteries. There was a china cabinet in the hallway, this beautiful piece of furniture was active. If we put any equipment near it, or a camera, something would happen. The house was cold even with the sun shining in, and it felt uneasy to sit there for any period of time. The family found themselves staying at a friend's house because they didn't feel safe in their own home. It was disruptive.

One afternoon the homeowner called me panic stricken. She said on video you could see a figure sitting on her daughter's bed while she was sleeping. The closet light was flickering on and off. I really think this was the last straw. Her children were more important than this home and they finally packed up and left. It was a slow process and they needed somewhere to go. They ended up staying with friends until they could find another place.

Our evidence was spot on and added to what she already had on her own camera. The homeowner finally packed up and left, but she left the china cabinet behind. The most powerful evidence was as they were leaving, the figure in the back of the house was looking out the window of her daughter's room watching them go.

We visited two of the homes that form part of the triangle, but the other residents claim they have seen things too. Another family did move in, but the last time I drove past that house it looked empty once again. So, what could have been causing the activity in this area? We may never know. It's safe to say that it's active and will likely remain that way. As for my clients, things have been okay since they moved, and it's been my hope that it stays that way for them.

Spirit entity in daughter's window at back of house

Chapter 20

Shiloh Road

W ay out on a road that never seems to end, with high grass and shrubs lining the entire road, beautiful and perfect, sits the last house on Shiloh Road. The house looked like it had been sitting unkempt for a while. It did not appear like anyone was living there, but there was.

A family, *so I thought*. They stayed in one room of the sprawling home, but another room was set up as a nursery. When they first reached out to me it was just to discuss some strange things that were going on in the home. Sara stated that they could smell coffee in the kitchen when nobody was in there, and the TV turned on and off by itself

When I arrived, the wife was happy to see me, but her husband came across as unsure. For their privacy I will call them John and Sara. The wife appeared fearful, and her husband was in denial that anything was wrong. He was not willing to accept what was happening. He said, "This is my damn house, and no ghosts are going to make me leave." He was angry to say the least. His wife was the one who wanted me to come out.

I could see that Sara wanted to speak with me, so I asked her what was going on. She looked at John and started to talk. She said the house has a few acres, and they recently borrowed a tractor to clear out the back of the property.

There was a swing set out there, I noticed it right away. As they were clearing the property they came across a small graveyard of five children's tombstones dating back to the early 1800s. They were shocked. She had enough.

I went there to talk, not really to investigate. I walked around, and I do keep equipment with me. I used the K2 meter to take a reading of the home around appliances and plugs, just looking for anything. I got nothing until I got to the back of the house. The K2 meter went straight to red and held there. I felt off. I walked back to the living room and I began to feel better. John looked at me and asked, "Did you feel it?" I said, "Yes, I did." Sara offered me coffee and I spent a few hours there.

Before I left, a little girl appeared and led me to her bedroom. In her room when I looked out the window I could see the grave site that had been hidden by the tall grass. *This couple had no children.* This child appeared to be in physical human form.

Spirits can appear in human form and there is a physical component. They can choose how they want to appear, and often choose a form similar to how they appeared in life. Spirits are more than energy.

This whole situation was odd from the moment I got

there. You can't make this stuff up even if you try. I offered to come back and investigate with my team; they were all for it.

After a month of trying to reach the homeowners, I decided to take a drive out to the house. I discovered the house was empty, the grass was tall and a "For Sale" sign was in the front yard. I was shocked, like, what happened here? I called the real estate agent on the sign and asked a few questions. This is where it gets crazy. She told me the couple moved out and it was a sudden move. I felt like I already knew why. I told the agent they were so nice, and their daughter was just adorable.

The agent said, "Daughter?" I was like, "Yes, the little girl." She then replied, "They didn't have any children." I was numb, it got really quiet, I did not know what had happened here. I asked, "Are you sure?" She said, "Yes." Honestly, I don't know what happened that night at the house on Shiloh Road. I don't even know how to explain it without it sounding crazy. To this day it's still mind boggling to me.

Chapter 21

The House in the Woods

T ucked away on a large piece of land in the woods sat a home. Looking at it from the outside you might think, *what could be wrong?* Once you walked inside you could just feel it. You *knew* something wasn't right. Things were happening at all hours of the day and night. Doors were opening and closing on their own. The homeowners were exhausted from no rest.

The homeowner always wondered if she carried something with her. She had a troubled past, and this all led to severe depression and a feeling of being trapped and doomed. This started in December 2020, a rough time for many. Being locked down in this situation led to feelings depression more than ever.

Our investigation there turned out to be an active one. We saw doors opening and closing. We heard voices in the house and saw lots of shadow figures. There was a grave out back and a Native American Burial Mound about 15 feet from the door. There was an alarm that repeatedly went off in the home as if someone passed in front of it, but nobody was there. The windchimes were ringing on a still, windless night. The animals were also reacting.

The homeowner's mother, BW, was particularly spiritual. Her Pentecostal religion had given her the ability to speak in tongues, known as the language the devil cannot understand. This is how Pentecostals speak to God. She spoke it a lot as she felt she needed to. She believed something evil was there trying to destroy her family.

It was the holidays, and we were to return after Christmas. The issues continued and the homeowner's depression deepened. Sadly, BW passed away unexpectedly. She had been the protector of the home. I was devastated to have lost such an amazing woman. She was a powerful soul. Her light went out and the months to follow brought sadness and more issues for the family. I became attached to BW, we connected. She knew that I understood what was going on in that house and she wanted her family safe. She trusted me. I could read her, and she could read me without saying a word. Rest in peace, BW, your spirit lives on and you are truly missed.

The homeowner has requested that we come back, and I plan to return to this home soon. The activity we observed on the first visit is still ongoing. I ran into her at a local store and she told me about her grandbabies seeing things and asking why the lights flash. What do you tell small children? The main thing here is to feel safe no matter what.

She is doing all she can to hold it together, but I do know this much, they are ready to leave. The homeowner's only fear is that whatever this is may follow her. She has questioned if whatever this is had followed her from a previous location once already.

I have no doubt that the mother is still there; she had quite a powerful soul. I believe she still protects the home and her loved ones. I am hopeful that we can resolve these issues and get more answers for this family and bring some peace to their lives.

Chapter 22

The Ninth Floor

The Biltmore Hotel in Miami is rumored to be a haunted hotel. I didn't know that on my first visit. Built in 1926, it was a place where the rich and famous hung out. In 1929 during prohibition a gangster named Thomas "Fatty" Walsh was shot and killed on the 13th floor after a dispute with another mobster. This spawned the first rumors of the hotel being haunted.

In 1952 the hotel was converted into a military hospital and saw a lot of death. It is no surprise that people say this hotel is haunted. The hospital closed in 1968 and the hotel sat abandoned for years.

In 1983 renovations began to turn it back into the beautiful hotel that it is today. The construction crews reported seeing all kinds of odd things. Tools would disappear and reappear in another location.

After reopening the hotel, there are stories out there that say a young mother fell to her death trying to save her young son who had climbed up on the balcony railing of their room. Another story is that of a married woman who was caught by her husband in bed with her lover. The husband killed them both. There have been many other deaths at the Biltmore and a lot of rumors about certain floors being more active than others. Again, I didn't know about any of these stories when I first stayed there.

I was around fifteen years old and I was living it up. Miami's nightlife was a blast. My father, my uncle, and their friends stayed here all the time. I was already living in Florida with my mother, but this was *my* time when my father visited me. We stayed in the penthouse of this hotel for a week straight that year.

I remember being in that elevator and going up to the penthouse and stopping on the ninth floor. The door opened, but no one was there. At first it seemed like just elevator issues, but it was a lot more frequent. The housekeeper told us "Oh, it's nothing, just the ghost on the ninth floor." I thought she might be joking, but I wasn't sure. Something felt odd on the ninth floor. My father and the other adults blew it off, but not me. I'd been curious about the paranormal since I was a child.

This hotel was huge and there was a lot to explore. The halls were long and the place was like a palace. I had fun running around this place. I took the elevator to the ninth floor — of course I did — because the words of the house-keeper had my curiosity in full swing.

When I saw the housekeeper again I said hello to her and

I asked her if she was just kidding about the ghost. She replied, "no" and walked down the hall and pointed to the room. She said, "It all started here in this room." I asked what happened, but she would not say. While on the ninth floor I encountered the spirit of a young girl. I wanted to know more about this room. I couldn't go in, but my curiosity got the best of me.

As I got older I had a few more chances to return to this hotel. It had gone through a second renovation by that time, but I still had weird feelings here. I never knew why every time I took the elevator it stopped on the ninth floor. To this day, I've never known why, but I always sense the young girl here. It was later I realized maybe it was something else, maybe a warning of things to come. I just have that sixth sense, I can't explain it.

Things have happened like this my whole life, such as going somewhere and seeing spirit, or seeing numbers and trying to figure out what they mean. The number nine always seems to mean something to me, from the first time I visited this location, until I was old enough to go there alone. I never entered that room, but there is a nine on the door. The ninth floor to me was symbolic in ways I may never understand. My dad died in 1999 — you read that right — and this whole nine thing came to a head for me.

As I write these pages, I realize that numbers have a symbolic meaning. As far as the ghost on the ninth floor is concerned, I may never know. One thing for sure, I always enjoyed my visits there. This location holds a special place in my heart and memories of times I had with my father.

Chapter 23

The Ward

It was a small home tucked behind trees in a residential neighborhood. The homeowner was a single woman with her dog. She was always on her computer, she loved music and had a great stereo system. One day while she was working on her computer she started to notice sudden interruptions in her equipment. Her stereo would have voices coming through the speakers. She initially thought it was radio interference. She really did not think much of it. This continued to happen, so she started to keep track of each occurrence. She heard voices coming through her speakers that were not from the computer or stereo.

She reached out to me and asked if we could come and check it out. I was not sure. Based on what I was told, it didn't seem like much. I went because I couldn't say one way or another until I saw it for myself. We set up a time and went to the home. Like I said, it was a small house. I could not understand what else could be causing that noise.

She sat down at her desk while my team checked the home and did a baseline check. As we stood there voices started coming from the stereo. They were muffled but we could hear them, along with a lot of static. About fifteen minutes into this a full sentence came through and it included the client's name, then you could hear nothing but static. I was shocked. There was nothing to cause this. The computer then shut down and turned back on. All of a sudden, the stereo went up to full volume, it was so loud that we literally jumped. No one expected that to happen.

After three hours in this home we all stepped outside. Suddenly we saw the lights inside start to flash. *No one was inside*. We heard a loud blaring noise, so we went back in to investigate; it was the stereo. This literally went on all night, voices and static. We never really got to the bottom of it. After we left the activity continued.

About two years later the house was torn down and a newer home was placed there; same owner. Why was it torn down? Was it because of paranormal activity? No, but prior to it being replaced it was an active location. I have not heard anything more regarding the stereo, voices, or the computer relating to the new home. Was it tied to the house? I don't really know. It's possible, since the home had been occupied for many years prior.

On the same street way back in the woods is an old railroad and a postal building that looks like an old house. There are many relics as well. No doubt the area where this home was located had a past and a history before it became a neighborhood. As for the current home, it seems quiet for now.

I guess you can say that all my experiences have led me to this one place in my life. Being a paranormal researcher is very much a part of me.

Denise watching K2

Denise Burroughs

Denise listening to Spirit Box

Chapter 24

The Haunted Inn - Savannah, Georgia

I have visited Savannah many times and it never disappoints. There is a strong history here and it's known as an active city. I had gone to Savannah for my wedding anniversary, rather than a case. I had assumed that most everything in the city of Savannah was haunted.

I stayed at the Foley House Inn, and I really had no idea of the full history behind this place. The current Foley House was built over the ashes of a home destroyed by the Great Savannah Fire of 1889. I was unaware of the alleged murder at the Foley House and the skeleton that was found behind a wall here during renovations. It was definitely active at night and turned out to be one of the most haunted bed and breakfasts in the area.

It was cold and windy, after all it was January in Savannah. I thought I was going to freeze to death. The wind was unreal. To be honest, I did not plan to stay in something haunted. This was my anniversary, I wasn't really looking for ghosts per se, but as it turned out this inn was full of ghostly fun.

We stayed in a gorgeous room with a beautiful bath and a four-poster bed. As night fell, things changed. Our first night there, while sleeping I heard the door handle rattle as if someone was trying to enter our room. I ignored it, figured it would go away on its own. It didn't. The next day we decided to go visit the city. As we entered the hallway, I smelled smoke. No one was there and there was no smoke anywhere. I didn't think much of it until later when I found out that a fire took place at this location.

The staircase was breathtaking, and the architectural design of this inn is so beautiful. There weren't many guests at the inn due to the weather in January. We went down to get coffee and to grab a bite to eat. I turned my head because in the mirror in front of me was a woman in period clothing. She had walked by and when I looked back she was gone. I was fascinated by what was going on at the inn.

We went out and spent most of the day checking things out. There were ghost tours at night. Of course I was going, just praying the wind would stop. We were doing some shopping and ran into a man downtown. He asked if we were having a good time and inquired as to where we were staying. The man asked if we had any visitations. I smiled and turned my head. As I looked back, he had disappeared. It was crazy.

We returned to the inn around dinnertime. It was quiet while we were getting ready to go back out for the evening. We needed ice, so I went into the hallway where I noticed a lady on the stairs. I said hello, and then she vanished. I remember speaking to the housekeeper and she asked if I met the lady. I told her "Yes, I believe I did." She just nodded her head.

Our visit at the Foley House Inn was truly enjoyable, it was a great time. I experienced a lot of unusual paranormal activity. As we were checking out, other guests were talking about similar experiences in the breakfast area. The staff themselves have also heard many odd stories from guests about the ghost on the stairs and the rattling doorknobs and agreed that strange things happen here.

Cool breezes, shadows, and apparitions; could all this be related to the murder that occurred here years ago? Or the fire? I really don't know. I would like to go back sometime and visit those who walk the halls of this beautiful historic inn.

Room at the Haunted Inn

Chapter 25

The House on Madison Street

Rome, New York is in the foothills of the Adirondacks in upstate New York. A lot of the homes are well over a hundred years old. My father lived in one of these homes and as a child I visited a time or two. I remember the summer that I spent in the house on Madison Street. My stepbrother at the time was just a baby in diapers, so it was just me and a few friends in the neighborhood. I spent a lot of time outside, as I didn't like the house. I always found a way to stay out of there by going to see my cousins who lived an hour away. I spent as much time as I could with them.

When you're a child you tend to let your imagination run away with you. My dad did not believe in all this stuff, but when you see a ball roll down the hallway by itself it's hard to ignore. To prove a point, I placed the ball in the same spot and it did nothing. But who was going to believe me? I was just a kid.

My father was a night owl and stayed up late every night. The floors always creaked when you walked on them, they were real old wood floors. Sometimes you could hear them creak when nobody was awake in the house, as though someone was walking on them. That was creepy. Other things have happened here as well, like the TV turning on and off by itself.

There was an attorney's office downstairs so you had to be quiet; they could hear everything that was said upstairs. One night after the attorney's office closed, you could hear all kinds of noises downstairs. I asked my dad, "What was that?" He replied, "It's just the old pipes." Yeah, right! I didn't believe him.

I haven't forgotten the eerie things that occurred in that house. I never really liked to talk about it much. I could hear full conversations near the attic crawl space. There was a small door that opened to this area; it was dark and creepy. One day I went in too far and the door started to close by itself. I never did that again. The voices I was hearing at this time in my life were the beginning of things to come. I identified my imaginary playmate years earlier as something more than what my mother thought.

I really don't know what was in this house on Madison Street, but it was enough to get my attention. My father didn't admit it, but deep down I think he knew, especially knowing he turned the TV off, but walked back in the room and it was back on.

My visit to Rome was short lived because I had to return home to Florida. It was many years later, after my father moved out, that he admitted things had happened there. He refused to speak about it. He was just old school Italian. He did not believe in Ghosts. Maybe that was why he was always gone, because he felt the same way. At the time he would just never admit the weird stuff that happened on Madison Street. However, I do know after my visit there that summer I was certain my dad was living in a haunted house.

Chapter 26

The House on Wright Road

This quaint home is located in a quiet neighborhood. It seemed like any other home, *but was it?*

When the homeowner and her son first started to experience odd things, they just blew it off as nothing. As time went on the odd experiences continued to increase. They saw weird lights, there were odd smells, and shadow figures. They both became worried that something else was going on. Was this just their imaginations running wild? Was it contributing to the mental health issues of the homeowner's son who had served in the military? What was happening here?

I was called to this location and was asked to investigate claims of ongoing unusual phenomena in the home. We spent three hours at this home and discussed that her son was having a hard time. The home was active, mostly in one room, but the son's room also showed activity.

Her son would stay up for hours hearing noises and

seeing dark shadows in his room. I never doubt people's stories until I can confirm or debunk it. The son struggled for a year or more dealing with the ongoing tension of what he was experiencing in the home. We finally put cameras up to monitor the space the best we could without invading his privacy. We placed a protective symbol in his room on the wall.

Everything quieted down in that space, but the energy made it outside of that area into other parts of the home. The room next to the son's was a different story. During our investigation we had several events occur on EVP and the spirit box. The best evidence we captured was from a ball that was used as a trigger toy, and a spirit who answered to Mr. Wilson. It was amazing how it touched the ball and made it go off. The spirit box went off when questions were asked. The spirit seemed friendly and willing to respond to all our questions.

It was about two years before we went back there. The activity continued in the home, you could feel the energy. We got strong EVPs, including images of something right in front of the camera and the SLS. This was the same room we spoke to Mr. Wilson in a couple of years earlier. One side of the home was cold, the other side was a normal temperature. Shadows often moved around; they were caught on camera in other rooms.

I was standing in the living room using the spirit box when I asked a specific question. Right after I asked that question my bag immediately fell over on my feet. All of this was caught on camera. I was told the homeowner's son is doing better and there's been no more activity in his room since we placed the protection symbol there.

The homeowners have made some sort of peace to be happy and enjoy their home. They don't feel threatened, and I don't think whatever it is was ever a bad thing. I think Mr. Wilson pops in every now and then and anything else that's there, for now, is harmless.

A couple of weeks after our second investigation, things started up once again. Strange lights in the window, shadows, and cold spots. The homeowner chose to stay and continues to live in the house. We do plan to return at some point to visit the location on Wright Road.

Chapter 27

The House at 161

T he house at 161 was not your ordinary house. It was built in the 1930s. It just had a way of drawing you in, there literally was no escaping that once you saw it. That's how this client felt, she was pulled right into it. To protect the family's privacy we will call the homeowners "Julie" and "Ron."

She had lived in this home for five years and it was great at first, but that all changed. As time went by she noticed that something just felt odd. My client was told several stories about a baby who was buried in the late 1800s to early 1900s at what would now be the beginning of the driveway. Research was done and through historical records we can confirm that a grave exists under what is the present driveway

Is it possible the home was sitting on a grave site from years ago? It's possible. Julie, the homeowner, noticed little things had started to happen; doors closing and lights flickering. She really did not think much of it at the time. It was an older home with all the creaks and settling that older homes have.

She told me later that the original homeowner had died in the home. He was the one who had built the house. I did my own research as well, and it clearly verified everything that Julie had told me. She didn't start to get concerned until one day when she was eating her dinner and a glass and dish flew off the counter, hit the floor, and shattered into a million pieces. She was upset and it totally shook her.

Julie didn't live alone, she had a husband and a daughter that stayed there with her two grandchildren. Over time things changed in the home and the activity became more intense. One afternoon her grandson was in the hallway talking to someone. She thought it was his sister he was talking with, but when she peeked around the corner there was no one there. She waited a bit and heard giggling. She looked again, and again, nothing. Her grandson continued his conversation. She watched as he rolled a ball down the hallway, only for it to roll back. No one else was in the hallway but her grandson.

Julie's daughter got concerned. The children were having nightmares and were talking into thin air. This went on for about two months and she decided to take the children out of the home for good. Julie and her husband also began to have issues.

Julie's husband, Ron, was a quiet man. He started to become agitated by Julie's claims of having visitors in the home. It was bad enough that her daughter left with the children. Ron had suggested that they just move out. Julie refused that suggestion. As time went on, she had gotten so wrapped up in this house that she didn't care anymore.

The activity grew even more; shadow figures, voices, and lots of movement within the home. She would stay up late just to watch the chandelier swing back and forth in her living room. She was mesmerized by it. She knew something was wrong, but she stayed. Ron was not the same, and the marriage started to fall apart. Julie called me and said, "Am I going to sound crazy by me telling you this?" I replied, "Not at all."

She began to tell me all that had been going on, I sat there and listened. Julie also sent me tons of videos. She started to isolate herself, it was just her and the house. Ron moved out; he couldn't take it anymore. He said to me "I've lost my wife, I have to go."

Julie became ill over time, unexplained issues like anemia and loss of appetite. She went to the doctor, but they couldn't find a reason for any of it. She lost a lot of weight and things were getting worse. We made a plan for me to go there, and we Facetimed a lot. My biggest concern was her health. Things went downhill fast. As we spoke, she showed me a video of things that were occurring. The chandelier started swinging. On video there was faint shadow movement in the kitchen area. On the recordings you could hear voices and moaning. It sounded like a house of horrors.

I did not realize the actual gravity of what was going on. I had only seen bits and pieces of the inside, however I did describe the outside of her home to a tee. She was shocked at how accurate it was.

I was supposed to see her one week from our last conversation. I did not hear from her and the appointment time had passed. She finally called, she was in the hospital incredibly ill. The last thing she told me was, "I lost my family. I gave my soul to the house. There are too many. I can't fight it anymore." That was the last time I heard from Julie.

Fast forward to January 2023. I received a call from a woman who had moved to the same address and location. She was also drawn to this home, just like Julie. Her life unraveled within five years. Is this a fluke? Is the home at 161 claiming another family? Only time will tell.

The current homeowner is ill and having major issues, too private for this book. A home she loved from afar and had moved to from another state is now causing her a lot of grief. She hates it and wants to move out and never look back. She just prays her family can survive long enough to leave. My conversation with the new owner ended just like Julie's. I hope to hear from her soon.

When EVP sessions were done from outside, it was active. The new homeowner heard giggling. She asked whomever it was to stop and to leave. She never heard it again.

There has since been a murder in the home. It is still an ongoing investigation, so that information cannot be shared at this time. It has forever changed the lives of the residents at 161.

Chapter 28

A Haunted Brothel

A brothel. Is that what I said? Yes, a brothel. It dates back to the late 1800s or early 1900s. On the threshold of the doorway is a plate that says "opera house." I cannot confirm that it once was an opera house, but I was able to confirm it was indeed a brothel. I use this building for a lot of different things, including events.

I filmed a web series there back in 2019, and the location did not disappoint. During filming I was overcome to the point where I had to leave the room. The cameraman was watching the entire thing unravel. It all started when we were doing a session and filming in one area of the building that was highly active. The equipment was going wild. All of a sudden I got a horrible headache and felt dizzy at the same time. At that moment my teammate, Chris, had an orb go up his side and he got severe chills. The camera caught the orb and his reaction. It was crazy because we were not even looking at each other during the filming. This building does not have any electricity, so we had placed lights in the hall-way. Suddenly the lights started going on and off.

We have always seen tall, dark shadows in the hallway and it's always in the same exact spot. I have taken guests into this building, and some can't even stay in it for more than five minutes before they have to leave. There is something here within this building, it's just not clear what, or whom, it is.

This brothel is located in a small town that was once known as an outlaw town. It has seen a lot of deaths, literally in front of its door. There used to be a tree in front of the door known as the "hanging tree." In the past it used to be a dirt road and there was a saloon downstairs from the brothel.

If you committed a crime you were hung from the tree out front. The history is hard to find, so a lot of this is shrouded in mystery. Most of the buildings where the brothel sits are all connected. They all have activity. There used to be a business downstairs where the saloon once was. I was told by the occupant that footsteps could be heard moving about upstairs at all hours, but most often between 7:30 and 8:00 p.m. *I am the only one with a key.*

Was there a gunfight here in the past? Did someone die in the brothel or the saloon? I don't know, but many were hung from that tree and died due to the crimes they committed. All of this took place in front of the brothel in this town. I will continue to investigate here, film, and share the location with others as long as I have access to this this cool place in history.

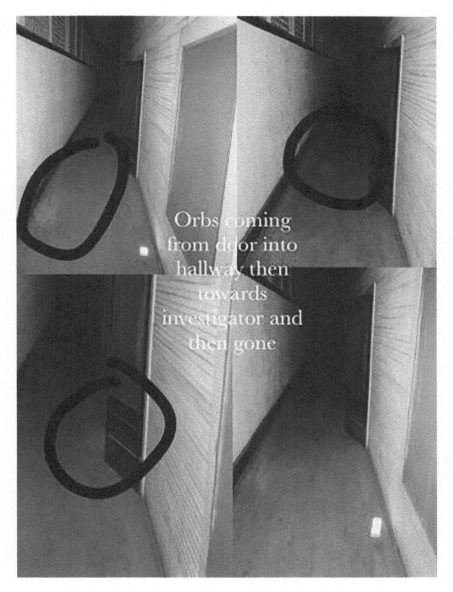

Orbs coming from door into hallway, then toward investigator, then gone

Denise Burroughs

Equipment showing activity

Chapter 29

The O'Quinn Drug Company

Construction of this two-story building was started in 1905 and completed in 1910. Barney O'Quinn, Sr. opened the O'Quinn Drug Company in 1911. This building remained a pharmacy until several years ago.

I investigated this location and I've researched the stories that were told to me. We visited the upstairs portion of the building. I had been told of a man who allegedly was shot and fell to his death. Oddly enough, one of the windows was boarded up. It was eerie in there. It was like time stood still, beautiful architecture, high ceilings. Everything was large and grand back in the day.

We climbed a narrow staircase to the top floor and spent two and a half hours collecting evidence and gathering photos. We did get a picture of a man by the window, I can't say for sure who that was. Our names were called out via the spirit box. It was eerie.

A few months earlier, before this case, one of my team

members passed away. We dedicated this investigation to him. It was our first investigation since the pandemic. It was weird investigating without him. He was on my team for over five years. I had the urge to ask if he was there, only because my batteries died as soon as I started. He used to joke with me about the batteries all the time. We replaced tons of batteries. I asked if he was there. Seconds went by and his name came across the spirit box plain as day, then my husband's name, then mine. I got chills. I knew with everything in me he was there during this case. We took our last picture and caught a photo of a man that looked just like our former teammate. He had on the same shirt he was wearing a month before he passed in a family Christmas photo.

It was a difficult investigation, so many emotions that night, but he reassured us he was present. I know he will always be with us as we travel and investigate. I dedicated this book to my friend and teammate, Mitchell Kingston. He made every case fun, even when we were scared out of our minds. He always knew what to say, and on the night of this investigation he let us know he was still there with us in spirit.

O'Quinn Drug Company

Chapter 30

The Train to Nowhere

The train to nowhere, literally nowhere. There's no way to explain the sound of a train rolling down the track, the sound of the locomotive chugging, the sound of its horn blaring, yet nothing. And then just like that, it's gone.

I have always called it the "ghost train." It's mysterious. It comes out of nowhere and then it's gone. The track exists tucked back between the trees in this quiet neighborhood on tracks that are still used by modern day trains. Nothing can prepare you for the sound of a train coming, only to have it vanish into thin air.

It's simply a mystery, or is it? I've been stopped at the railroad crossing and I've heard the train coming down the track, train horn and all. I have listened to the sounds, I have watched the train come and go.

I am not sure why this happens. The area has a history. The tracks are old, so is this whole area. I realized long ago

148

that nothing in this world is easily explained. I call it a freaky phenomenon, one that no matter what you do, you just can't explain it. It's a mystery. Catching it on camera would be amazing. Maybe one day I will get lucky, but for now I will just wait for it.

Chapter 31

Robert The Doll

Probably one of my most interesting visits was to the Keys. I've been there many times because Florida is my home. As a paranormal researcher I have always been fascinated by the history of Florida and, of course, the Keys. I have spoken on the subject of haunted dolls and objects in this book, but I was always fascinated by one doll in particular, and that is Robert the Doll. He is one of a kind.

Robert has a strong and well-documented history making him one of the oldest residents of Key West. He is said to be over 117 years old. He is dressed like a sailor and is said to be possessed by the spirit of a young child. Much has been said about Robert and his story and how he became what he is today. There are many people who don't know anything about him.

On a trip to the Keys with some friends I visited the museum where Robert lives. I also did some sightseeing and paid a visit to the historic Key West bed and breakfast known as The Artist House. Although Robert is now in a museum, The Artist House was his original home. The story goes that Robert the Doll had his own room in the attic, complete with furniture. It's a beautiful place with a history like no other. This island home has been operating as a bed and breakfast since 1978, it was a cool place to visit.

When I did visit Robert there was a strong feeling of being watched, at least for me there was. Robert sits in a large glass case. I saw so many people taking pictures of him, and many just standing and staring at him.

I did my homework before visiting him. They say that you must ask Robert's permission to take a photo, or it won't turn out. I asked him if I could take a picture of him. The photo was a little blurry. It was many years ago, I don't have that photo or camera anymore. I wish I did, but maybe it was for the best.

My friends took pictures of Robert, but they did not ask for his permission. None of their photos came out at all. All I know is that it was a cool experience for me and my friends that weekend in the Keys. My friends knew I had a major interest in the paranormal, but they didn't really understand it.

I have not been back to the Keys in a long time. It's crazy because I live in the State of Florida. You would think I'd visit more, but a lot has happened over the years, hurricanes and things like that. I would like to go back someday.

I own many haunted dolls and I was lucky enough to find a doll maker overseas who made me a beautiful replica of the original Robert the Doll. Although he is not haunted like the original, it's kind of cool to know I'm one of only a few who have a doll like him in my collection. My replica of Robert sits in my paranormal office on display in an old rocking chair dating all the way back to the 1800s. It's more than fitting for him. He is not haunted, but he is surrounded by haunted friends that I have collected over the years.

My Robert is on display for those that visit me, and a lot of people are not aware of who he is. I did do an episode on Robert on my *Haunted Florida* podcast. After all, he is one of the most haunted dolls in America. I look forward to visiting the Keys again and making a stop to visit Robert at the museum.

Chapter 32

The Haunting of the St. Augustine Jail

A few years back my team and I traveled to St. Augustine. We did a two-and-a-half-hour exclusive investigation in the jail. It was just us there, no guides. It was a private investigation. The jail is well known to be haunted. On the night of the investigation, we set up in different places. Me and a couple of other members were in the women's maximum security prison area. It was attached to the men's side.

As we were standing there I suddenly felt sick to my stomach. I was told by a tour guide that another well-known paranormal investigator had the same thing happen to him in the same spot during the filming of a popular TV show. The tour guide asked if I was okay and if he could just watch.

Our equipment was going crazy in the jail cell area. I could ask questions and would get repeated responses. I somehow felt drawn to the name Mae. I'm not sure why, but when I asked questions and asked if I was speaking to Mae there was a clear response back. The K2 meter and REM-POD were totally lit up.

Somehow I felt like Mae was with child, that's what it felt like to me. As we moved through the jail a photo was taken of me and my daughter, who had joined us that night. Behind us in the photo was the shadow of a man in an old police officer's hat and uniform. The others felt something tapping them on the shoulders. We heard sounds coming from upstairs and saw shadow figures throughout this location. As we looked outside the second story window to the gallows, the wind started to blow. It was an eerie scene that night. We continued to investigate the quarters of Chief Perry's office.

We have what sounds like a man's voice on a voice recorder from this location. We got a lot of evidence from the St. Augustine Jail. So much that the evidence is located at the San Marcos Welcome Center in St. Augustine.

I think I should mention that at the moment when we saw the police figure, there was a voice captured that said, "I'll kill you." That evidence is also at the Welcome Center.

As we were leaving we did a dowsing rod session, it too was active. I felt we needed to close our end of it down because I felt strongly that something wanted to leave with us.

Before we left I went back to the women's cell, sat on the floor, and said goodbye to Mae. I told her I would be back. She responded many times as the REM-POD flashed many colors, mainly green. I felt bad in a way, I felt she had a story to tell. I assured her I would return.

I plan to return to this location, as well as the lighthouse. It was a great night for Paranormal Investigators of North

Florida. All this evidence is on our Facebook page in video form, as well as at the San Marcos Welcome Center in St. Augustine. If you were ever in doubt about the history of this town, doubt no more. St. Augustine lives up to its reputation as one of the most haunted locations in Florida.

Jail cell

Denise Burroughs

Shadow on the left is spirit of old time guard, note the hat

Chapter 33

Madison Books

M adison Books is located in the sleepy town of Madison, Florida at 254 SW Range Avenue. Madison was settled by cotton planters in 1838. The building where this bookstore is located was built around 1920 as far as we can tell. It is located adjacent to the building that housed the historic Smith Drug Store, which opened in 1904 and served the community for 70 years. Not many records survive from that time. The only history that we can find of this specific location comes from local old timers who say that the building may have been a general store at some point. It was later a clothing store, part of a livestock feed store, and then a dress shop.

I got involved after a chance meeting with the store owner where she reported some unexplained things happening in the building. I was told that they frequently come to work in the morning and find a few books on the floor in front of the shelving units for no apparent reason. They have all smelled old-fashioned perfume wafting through the back room that disappears after a minute.

One employee reported feeling a hand touch her arm when she was working alone. Footsteps that sound like they belong to a child running upstairs have been heard during business hours. There are reports of cold spots from time to time, and a visible shimmer or warping in the air. An employee that works in their upstairs space was encountering a lot of activity. He reported the odd sensation of tingling on the back of his neck and his hair standing on end. There were knocking and scraping noises coming from a wall that doesn't connect to anything. When things started falling off the table in front of him for no obvious reason, he was afraid. They needed answers.

My team and I came out to do an investigation in May of 2024. We walked the space with our K2 meters and picked up some strong readings. In the upstairs space our equipment detected temperature changes. We went back downstairs and set up the Trip Wire. When we started asking questions it lit right up in response. It's a pretty active location.

We did a lengthy spirit box session and asked a lot of questions. The responses were in a female voice, and we identified a female spirit by the name of Amanda. During the session we learned that she died in 1940. She indicated that she used to frequent the store that was located here back then.

I asked why she drops books on the floor and Amanda told us that there is the spirit of a two-year-old child here too. The child has no relation to her, and she doesn't know why the child is here, but that she reads to it. I asked if she always stays here or if she travels to other old buildings on the block. She indicated that she does not travel and that she is always here because she likes it.

We were seated in a circle around a table while doing the session and the Trip Wire was on the floor lighting up. Two of the people seated saw Amanda physically manifest near some bookshelves opposite the Trip Wire during our spirit box session. We always end a session by saying goodbye and thank you to the spirits. We got an audible response of "goodbye" from Amanda.

The owners don't mind the ghosts being here as long as they behave. I closed by letting Amanda know that as long as she does not cause harm she is welcome here. We let the owners know that if something changes and they need us we will come back. For now, everyone is coexisting just fine. If you are ever in Madison, Florida drop by Madison Books and visit Amanda.

Trip Wire session

Denise Burroughs

Denise using software to communicate with Amanda

Denise Burroughs

Orbs caught on camera

Chapter 34

The Horseshoe House

Horseshoe Beach is a small, quiet village at the end of Dixie County Highway 351. Today it is a thriving fishing community. The town was first settled in the 1800s. The land was originally owned by a lumber company. When the company ran out of timber to cut they began to urge their employees to move out. In 1935, C.C. Douglas and Burton Butler purchased the land for $324 and offered each resident squatter the lot he was living on for $10. Many of these settlers stayed on and worked as fishermen. The town of Horseshoe Beach was born, and it was incorporated by the residents in 1963.

I first got involved with this home after being shown a video that the homeowner's security cameras picked up while they were out. It looked like a person walking on the bottom left-hand corner of the screen. The homeowner wasn't sure what to make of it, but it went to the middle of the screen and disappeared, and then you could see an orb floating by. On our first phone call the homeowner told me the history of the home. Built in 1939 as a one-bedroom house, it has been added onto over the years. According to locals, in the past this home was owned by a drug smuggler. We could confirm that due to the coastline, drug smuggling thrived here in the '70s and '80s. One local told her a story about a freezer on the back porch of this home full of money. The homeowner has also been told that there may have been money buried on the property at one time. It was an old house with history to it.

When they first bought the house it seemed peaceful. They would hear sounds off and on, like a knock here and a bump there. It was an old house and they didn't think anything of it at the time. They would come out on weekends to work on the property, and they put a battery-operated clock on the wall. When they got back the following weekend the batteries would be dead. After several times they just stopped replacing them.

The house turned out to be quite active. When their oldest grandson was three years old, he had been playing in his bedroom and came into the living room and asked, "Nana, what color hair did your mom have?" She asked him "Why?" and he said, "Because there is a gray-headed woman back there talking to me." The homeowners went back to look and there was no one there.

About five years later their middle grandson, who was three years old at the time, was watching TV in the bedroom and came out to the living room saying, "Nana, there's a woman in there and she's mean." She asked what color hair the woman had and he said, "White." She checked the bedroom and no one was there.

A few years later their youngest grandson was playing in the bedroom and he came into the living room saying, "Nana, there's an old woman back there." Again, she asked what color her hair was, and he said, "White." When she went back there to look, no one was there.

Her husband was in his bedroom alone one night in bed and the next morning he said that he felt like something was getting into bed with him. He also heard banging noises coming from the attic and banging on the walls.

She used to keep a light on in the kitchen when she went to bed in case someone got up and needed to see. One night she decided to turn all the kitchen lights off when she went to bed. A few hours later she got up and went to the kitchen for something and the light over the sink was on. Another night she had been up watching tv and turned it off to go to another room to do some sewing. She started hearing voices and when she walked into the living room the tv was on again. When she told her family they didn't believe her. They assumed she forgot to turn the light and tv off.

A few weeks later in May 2021 when no one was at the house the door camera went off. Her husband hit the live record button and captured the video that I was shown prior to our first phone call. This home was active and they needed answers, so we made a plan to come out.

As soon as we walked in you could feel that something was there. The house showed activity right away. We placed a Trip Wire on the porch near the rocking chair and it moved.

When we arrived and started setting up our equipment the homeowner made a comment about her husband. The K2 meters immediately went to red. I asked her to repeat what she had just said, and the K2 meters went to red again. I asked her to keep talking and every time she mentioned her husband the K2s lit up red. Her husband was not there that night so I asked if she could call him and get him to come to the house. There is a female energy in the home. It seems to be attracted to the husband. We did a spirit box session and learned that the female spirit was from the 1800s and that the homeowner's husband had been the spirit's husband in another life. During the session on the front porch with the spirit box we clearly heard, "I hear his truck." Two minutes later the husband drove up. We got a lot of evidence that night.

We walked the perimeter of the property and captured a shadow against the wall and multiple images of children's faces outside. There is a graveyard nearby. When we were about to leave, we told the spirit on the porch with the rocking chair that we were going and thanked them. The spirit clearly said "good night" on audio.

The homeowner told us that the home was purchased based on a chance meeting and the sale happened quickly. Three days after they made the decision, the papers were signed. Sometimes the spirits make things happen like that.

Since our investigation the homeowner has reported ongoing activity. After we left that first night she experienced a cold feeling on her arm and later her leg and hip. She asked the spirit to leave her alone and let her sleep, and the feeling was then gone. Since then, they have caught orbs on camera and felt the sensation of being touched. She tells the spirits that she feels them and knows they are there, and asks to be left alone. It seems to help.

In August 2023, Hurricane Idalia hit Horseshoe Beach. The house didn't have any damage and power was restored quickly, so they stayed there, along with their daughter's family, while they all waited for the power to come back on at their primary residences. Her daughter had been in the kitchen and walked out to the dining room and said, "I have a cool feeling on the right side of my body." She also smelled something that reminded her of the hairspray an old woman would use. She then commented that it made her feel like it was her Granny, who is deceased.

This is still an active home and we plan to go back there to continue our investigation soon.

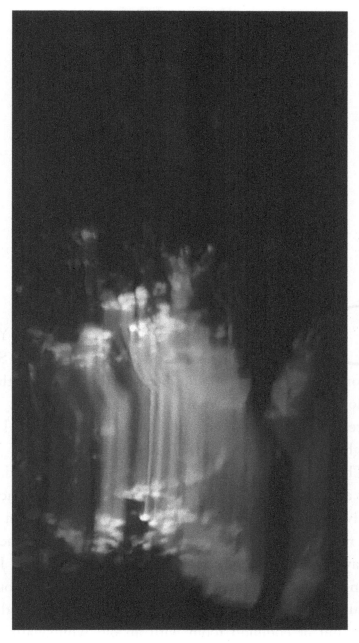

Child spirits

Chapter 35

The Sanitarium

David Howell Yates, M.D. opened his first Sanitarium in Madison, Florida in 1914. Dr. Yates brought the first electrostatic machine to the State of Florida. This was a portable shock-producing electrotherapeutic device commonly known as the medical battery. This device provided both direct and alternating current and was thought to cure a wide variety of ailments.

There was a fire in 1922 and the sanitarium burned. Dr. Yates abandoned this location and instead built a new facility on Livingston Street. The site of the 1914 sanitarium had been rebuilt at some point and operated as a medical facility or maybe an apartment or rooming house in the past. I am making an educated guess based on what we saw in the building, such as rooms labeled with numbers and what looked like some kind of common room with an old whiteboard with names. The whiteboard was invented in the mid-1950s, so we know it was operating as something after that time. We could not find reliable records for this address, which is common in these small towns.

This building is private property and we were invited to explore the space by the owner. At the time of our visit, it had been empty for many years and renovations were just beginning. It looked like a time capsule from another era. There was no electricity at the time of our visit, so we were prepared with lanterns just in case.

The moment you entered this building you could just feel an oppressive, heavy feeling. We were not inside for more than a few minutes when suddenly doors started slamming upstairs. One of our investigators is in law enforcement and proceeded to go up there and do a sweep of the building. There was no one there.

We went upstairs and explored each of the rooms. We saw visible shadow figures in some of the rooms and in the hall. I got strong readings on the K2 meter, so I laid the Trip Wire down near the top of the stairs at the entrance to the hall just to see what we would get. There was activity on both the Trip Wire and K2 meter. We got a lot of answers to our questions on that second floor. The eerie energy was everywhere up there. I could see it in the mind's eye.

At the far end of the hall, behind the last door on the left, there was a staircase that was wide enough for one person to fit at a time. It led down from the second-floor patient rooms to a locked door. We were able to unlock the door from the other side and it was a tiny office barely large enough to hold a desk and two people. We don't know the purpose of this room, but there was quite a bit of energy present. Could it have been a treatment room at one time? We don't know.

I decided to head back downstairs to explore the rest of the building. As we started to look around we were greeted with a large snake slithering across the floor, followed by a smaller one a minute later. I really don't like snakes. We were cautious walking the rest of the space.

I set up the Trip Wire inside the entryway because it was obvious there was a lot of spirit energy centered down there. As I said before, you could feel it the moment you walked in the door. I like to ask questions that are obvious. We know that it's a sanitarium. We know that there was likely death and a lot of bad things that happened. I look for a reaction to the questioning from the spirit or spirit energy that is still there. The line of questioning is important, it's not a trick question and it's not a stupid question. It's an obvious question, but I am looking for the answer to confirm what we already know. The Trip Wire was active and we got a lot of questions answered.

When I set up the spirit box there were two distinct voices speaking to us, one male and the other female. The female indicated that she was present when the sanitarium burned in 1922. When asked if Dr. Yates was there at the time she also said, yes. This spirit confirmed that there was a lot of suffering here and death here. I asked the male entity if he was Dr. Yates but did not get a conclusive answer. The male entity did indicate that he was also there at the time of the fire and that there was a lot of death that night.

We had to end the session for the evening for safety reasons. It was getting dark. Although we had lanterns, once we saw snakes in the building it was not a good idea to chance tripping over one in the dim lantern light and getting hurt. It was also really hot in the building. We will be returning to this location in the fall when the weather cools off. I look forward to coming back to do another spirit box session to see what we can learn about the spirits still residing here.

Denise Burroughs

Sanitarium

Denise Burroughs

Trip Wire activated

Denise Burroughs

Upstairs patient room

Denise Burroughs

Sanitarium upstairs hallway

Chapter 36

The Equipment

A lot of people have inquired about what kind of equipment we use. To be honest, if spirit wants to talk to you, you really do not need much. I always use a good video camera, a voice recorder, K2 meter, REM-POD, Trip Wire and dowsing rods. Believe it or not, I still use a cassette player because I have picked up some great stuff while using it. After all, it was the equipment choice back in the day and still is for some of us. I always use a spirit box for my spirit box sessions. I use a blindfold on a team member who helps listen and connect to what's being said.

DEFINITIONS:

K2 meter: The K2 meter(K-II) is an electromagnetic field meter. These devices are used to detect and measure any potential electromagnetic anomalies that may take place during a paranormal investigation. It is a tool for detecting spikes in the electromagnetic field (EMF).

SLS Camera: Structured Light Sensor Camera System. It captures video evidence of spirit forms during paranormal investigations that can't be seen with the naked eye. These forms are depicted as stick figures.

REM-POD: Radiating Electro-Magnetic Pod. It is a device designed to detect fluctuations in electromagnetic fields.

Spirit Box: Uses radio frequency sweeps to generate white noise with a frequency scan mode meant to detect EVPs and communicate with spirits giving entities the energy they need to be heard.

Laser Grid: Enables you to visualize anomalies as they occur in a room during a paranormal investigation.

Video Camera: Records images for later playback.

Cassette Recorder both digital and regular: A voice recorder is simply used to capture the audio of a location and for capturing EVPs, which are voices captured on recording equipment.

Trip Wire: Trip Wires come in varying lengths and are a string of microprocessor-controlled EMF sensors spaced at intervals. They emit several different colors when EMF fluctuations and spikes are detected. They are highly visible from all sides so that your group can see them.

Dowsing Rods: Dowsing rods, also known as divining rods, are used in ghost hunting to locate paranormal energy.

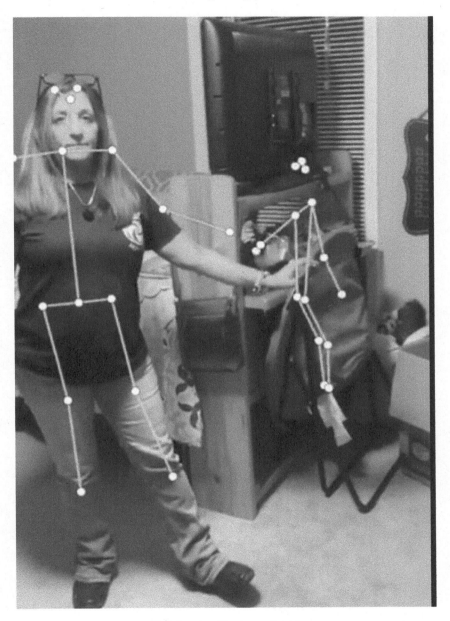

SLS showing Denise and spirit

Denise Burroughs

Spirit Box session

Conclusion

Over the years I have become known for doing in-home cases. People call and usually their first words are "I hope this does not sound stupid but..." Hey, nothing is stupid. Going to someone's home to help is an important thing that I take seriously. These people who reach out need answers. What they experience is real, and I think it's important to just listen. I have had people tell me that they waited to reach out, simply because they weren't sure if what they saw was real and didn't want to be judged. I don't want people feeling that way.

From the moment someone reaches out, I take the time to talk to them and allow them to tell their story fully. I always say, ask as many questions as you want. I've created a place here where people can feel at ease, even when they are terrified. I care about all my families. We build friendships. I have met some great people, all who have a different story to tell. I have met people that were skeptical and became believers really quick. The paranormal is a real thing and most of my clients have had real experiences. I am intrigued by all of it.

Sometimes it's not ghosts. There have been times when we have been called to a home and there was no evidence of the paranormal. Sometimes they just need to communicate their feelings, or they are hoping to hear from those who have passed. I believe that being there for someone who has lost a loved one when they needed clarity and understanding is such a privilege.

To me, it's a job like anything else. I decided when I started a team that I had to have compassion and understanding. To help people who have had these experiences you have to be able to relate to what they are going through. The only way to do that is to say, *I have been there, I get it. I know exactly what you are saying.* I have been asked many times if I think that I have helped people. I believe I have.

I get asked all the time "Do you go back?" The answer is, yes. Sometimes the issue is not resolved in one visit, so we will go back. I screen all my cases, and I talk to people before going out. I do my research and I ask for evidence, and most are good about it. They take pictures and record what they see and hear, and it helps a lot. So, yes, I have gone back once or twice. Sometimes even more, depending on the home, the client, and the need. I always leave letting them know we are just a phone call away. I don't want people to feel alone and lost in fear. I am honest if I can't deal with the issues, and I will find someone who can. For the most part we get it done, and that is what we like.

How do people find me? By word of mouth. If they are happy with you, they will talk about you to everyone. I would say I get literally hundreds of messages, and I get back to everyone. Like I said, it's a job.

Three years ago I acquired a local office. The office of Paranormal Investigators of North Florida is a hub for all the work that my team and I do. We do a lot of events and public appearances. Once a year I hold a paranormal workshop that allows people to come in and learn about our work, the paranormal, and discuss whatever they want to know. Our workshops appeal to a broad audience and attendees come from all walks of life, socio-economic backgrounds, and age groups. You can find our scheduled in-person events by following the Paranormal Investigators of North Florida Facebook page. The workshops fill up quickly.

Spiritual activity has touched many over the years. I have had a warm reception in this field, but many have paved the way for me. I think my team and I have done a great job. At times I feel like we are ghost therapists; one of my team members said that to me before a case and it rings true. I don't like to give people the impression that we can send people who have passed into the light. I feel that the soul must be ready. When it's ready, it will go. Many have unfinished business, as I call it. I treat the dead with the same respect as the living, that is really important.

We once did a case in a cemetery where I saw an image that has stayed with me for years. I saw a child in spirit form standing next to her tombstone. To this day it is the most surreal thing I have ever seen. Regardless of location, big or small, I believe the effects are the same. Although you may get more activity in a larger location, it's definitely on spirit's time. I don't think you are ever really prepared because every situation is different.

The paranormal journey is filled with many unknowns. However, no matter what may come, one thing is for certain: In the end we are all just stardust.

Conclusion

Conclusion

Denise reviewing evidence

Conclusion

Investigating spirit in Spirit Box session

Workshop lecture on paranormal

Conclusion

Paranormal Investigators of North Florida

Acknowledgments

ACKNOWLEDEMENTS

To the Reader,

I would like to express my deepest appreciation to my readers and followers of my paranormal journey. May you know how much you are appreciated and what a gift you are.

To My Mother,

Thank you for your wisdom and for teaching me to always trust my gut and to listen to the inner voice in my head. I will always be grateful for your guidance and support. You helped make me the woman that I am today.

To My Team Members,

Who help make what I do possible, and what we do together amazing. To those rare, beautiful friendships that change our lives forever, Ladonna Denmark and Chris Estes, I cherish you both. Thank you for being a part of this crazy ride.

To My Husband, Cliff,

Thank you for being my ride or die and for being the biggest supporter in my life. I could not have undertaken this journey without you.

To My Grandson, Wyatt

Who inspires me to look at the world with the wonder of a child and believe that everything is possible. I love you unconditionally and feel fortunate that you love crazy scary movies, Ghostbusters, and science fiction just like your GiGi.

To My Editor

I would like to thank my editor April Balsamo Davis for helping turn this book into a reality.

About the Author

Denise Burroughs is a paranormal researcher and medium who discovered her ability to communicate with the spirits at a young age. An accomplished businesswoman, she founded Paranormal Investigators of North Florida while studying Parapsychology.

Denise has investigated well over 100 unique paranormal cases during the last 25 years. She collaborated with the

Catholic Church in one of her extreme cases, resulting in the involvement of a demonologist.

Denise has been featured on *Haunted Hospitals* which aired on T&E and the Travel Channel. Listen to her podcast *Haunted Florida* on Spotify, Amazon, iHeart, Apple and Google.

Keep up with the investigations of Denise Burroughs and Paranormal Investigators of North Florida on Facebook https://www.facebook.com/ParanormalInvestigatorsOf NorthFlorida and YouTube https://www.youtube.com/@ paranormalinvestigatorsofn7594, as well as her Haunted Florida Facebook group https://www.facebook.com/groups/ 537536951283308. You can reach out to Denise at Haunt-edFloridaPodcast@gmail.com.

About the Editor

ABOUT THE EDITOR

April Balsamo Davis studied Communications, English, and Business, graduating in 1984. Her editing journey started in the public affairs department of a major market radio station in Miami. She has been editing the spoken word in the legal arena since 1985.

Currently she does freelance editing and proofreading with a focus on the genres of fantasy, horror, and memoir/nonfiction. She is also a staff editor for INKD Pub working on various anthologies.

abalsamo@inkdpub.com

232

Also by Denise Burroughs

Let's Eat

The Adventures of Willow Spider and Friends

The Story of the Day You Were Born

On Amazon worldwide:

https://www.amazon.com/stores/Denise-Burroughs/author/
BoD3QS7GPR

Also available on many worldwide outlets

Also by Inkd Pub

Anthologies

Spooky fiction series: *Noncorporeal*

Horror series: *Behind the Shadows*

Mystery series: *Detectives, Sleuths, and Nosy Neighbors*

Speculative fiction series: *Hidden Villains*

A variety of diverse anthologies full of short stories curated by dedicated editors.

www.inkdpub.com